How Is It with Your Soul?

Priscilla Pope-Levison and Jack Levison

United
Methodist
Women
FAITH · HOPE · LOVE IN ACTION

United Methodist Women
PURPOSE

The organized unit of United Methodist Women shall be a community of women whose purpose is to know God and to experience freedom as whole persons through Jesus Christ; to develop a creative, supportive fellowship; and to expand concepts of mission through participation in the global ministries of the church.

The Vision

Turning faith, hope and love into action on behalf of women, children and youth around the world.

Living the Vision

We provide opportunities and resources to grow spiritually, become more deeply rooted in Christ and put faith into action.

We are organized for growth, with flexible structures leading to effective witness and action.

We equip women and girls around the world to be leaders in communities, agencies, workplaces, governments and churches.

We work for justice through compassionate service and advocacy to change unfair policies and systems.

We provide educational experiences that lead to personal change in order to transform the world.

Contents

Participant's Guide

Introduction

At the close of John's Gospel, Jesus' disciples huddle together, scared to death of the leaders who had executed Jesus only a few days ago. The doors are locked tight until, in a single breathless moment, Jesus joins them. He greets them casually, as if he's just back from a walk in the park: "Peace be with you."

> *Shalom aleykem.*
> *Jambo.*
> *Annyeonghaseyo.*
> *Namastē.*
> *Osiyo.*
> *Hola.*
> *Hello.*
> *Aloha.*

Then the drama begins in earnest. With a simple, unceremonious word, Jesus commissions his flawed and frightened band of friends. He says hello again—"Peace to you"—and then, wham! "As the Father has sent me, so I send you" (John 20:21). Maybe these words are not quite as familiar as the Great Commission at the end of Matthew's Gospel—"All authority in heaven and on earth has been given to me. Go therefore and make disciples . . ." (Matthew 28:18-20)—but the gist is the same. Jesus, raised from the grave with fresh authority, commissions these friends who've stuck with him, more or less, to carry his word and his authority to the ends of the earth.

This is a heady call for those of us who have more than our share of daily preoccupations and commitments, even church commitments. But, truth be told, it is our primary call, the first commission of the risen Jesus, the greatest commission he would ever give. "As the Father has sent me, so I send you."

Our response to this commission might drive us to lock ourselves in the room—scared to death of Jesus' expectations and full of questions. How can we possibly live up to this commission? How can we conceivably accomplish Jesus' plans for us? How can we ever carry Jesus' life and work to earth's ends?

Look again at this private scene, this reunion of Jesus with his friends, and you'll see how: "When he had said this, he breathed on them and said to them, 'Receive the Holy Spirit'" (John 20:22).

He breathed on them. Jesus could spit on the eyes of the blind, lay his hands on the sick, have his feet caressed with hair and washed with tears, even wash his disciples' feet, but nowhere else in the Gospels does Jesus breathe on someone. Never before does this level of physical intimacy characterize the way he approaches those for whom he cares so deeply.

In fact, the Greek verb translated, *breathe on*, should be translated, *breathe in*. Jesus breathed *in* them—personally and intimately—the Holy Spirit. What Jesus does in the locked room looks very much like a kiss. Not a kiss on the cheek, like the betrayer's kiss, but a kiss on the mouth, by which the Spirit of one person passes to another. Jesus' inbreathing and their receiving the Holy Spirit is the same action, occupying the same brief moment in time.

The intimacy of this scene is heightened by the verb John chooses to convey the inbreathing of the Holy Spirit. It is the same verb used in Genesis 2:7 of the inbreathing of the first human being: "then the LORD God formed [*adam*] from the dust of the ground, and *breathed into* his nostrils the breath of life; and [*adam*] became a living being" (emphasis added). This is the kiss of life. This is our first breath.

When our daughter Chloe was a couple of years old, she'd climb onto my (Jack's) lap, stand unsteadily, set her small mouth full on over my nose, breathe deep—*and blow*. A full-force gale of toddler's breath. Whoosh. I'd feel my nose fill, my head swell, and her breath sneak out of my eyes, even. She'd giggle. I'd belly laugh. *Adam* in the garden. The breath of life breathed full-on into my face.

As God had breathed into the face of the first man, Jesus breathes now into the face of his disciples, and they, in turn, receive this Holy Spirit. He imparts this Spirit-breath, not at arm's length, but mouth to mouth, face to face, in the shared intimacy of friends reunited in a locked room.

Shalom. Hello. Aloha. We were standing in line at graduation this year, chatting about the Holy Spirit with a colleague who was born and raised in Hawaii. He told us that *aloha!* is onomatopoetic. It sounds like what it is: outbreathing that is, at one and the same time, inbreathing. Exhalation that is inhalation, too. How so? When a native Hawaiian is troubled and out of sync, our colleague explained, a friend leans in, forehead to forehead, and breathes out *alo-ha!* The breath—*ha!*—of the one in sync brings life, balance, grace to the one who is weak and out of whack. *Aloha! Shalom! Hello!* This custom illuminates Jesus' action with his frightened disciples: "When he had said this, he breathed *into* them and said to them, 'Receive the Holy Spirit.'"

The ability to nurture what we might call, in light of this story, commission and inspiration—the external and internal workings of faith—shapes how we answer the central question of this book, "How is it with your soul?" If your answer is, "I spend my days and nights giving and organizing and leading but can barely come up for breath," this book is for you. If your answer is, "I retreat to the quiet of a private devotional life but have set outreach aside," this book is for you. If your answer is, "I don't pay much attention to my spiritual life or Jesus' commission," this book is for you, too. This book will help you bring into balance the inner and outer dimensions of the Christian life.

We've organized this book around four verbs: *pray, learn, mentor,* and *transform.* The first two verbs—pray and learn—communicate the power of inspiration, receiving, inbreathing. We want you to see prayer and learning, not as two more obligations in life, two more responsibilities that weigh on your shoulders. We want you instead to pray and learn in ways that restore, revive, revitalize who you are. And we believe that, if you put into practice what you read in the first two chapters, you will develop habits that allow Jesus to lean in, forehead to forehead, and breathe the Spirit of life into you.

The last two verbs—mentor and transform—communicate the power of action, giving, reaching out. We want you to see mentoring and being active in transformation not as two more activities you are failing to do or do well. We want you instead to mentor others and become agents of transformation in ways that restore, revive, and revitalize our churches and our world. And we believe that, if you put into practice what you read in the last two chapters, you will develop habits that allow Jesus to lean out, hand to hand, and breathe the Spirit of life into others.

There is, in fact, a formidable synergy between the first two verbs—*pray* and *learn*—and the last two—*mentor* and *transform*. Mentoring, for example, may mean praying and learning alongside someone else so that he or she can become a more mature disciple of Christ. Your faith, of course, will grow more vibrant as well in the process. Transformation, too, grows out of prayer and learning, capturing a vision from scripture and listening for a word that sends you to precisely where God would have you be, where your prayer and learning and mentoring and transformation will be effective in the grand scope of God's design.

Right now you are opening the pages of this book for the first time. We hope, as you close it, that you'll be able to answer the question, "How is it with your soul?" with a resounding, "It is *well* with my soul!" The question itself, "How is it with your soul," comes from the Methodist class meeting, which has been called the "sinews of Methodism."[1] The class meeting soon became the heart of the early Methodist movement in England, providing the most basic setting of spiritual formation. It was brought to North America by lay Methodists as they emigrated, providing the foundation of the movement here nearly a decade before Wesley sent over itinerant preachers to foster the growth. And the class meeting took off! By 1815, more than seven thousand Methodist class meetings were up and running.[2]

Week by week, Methodists, according to Wesley, would "speak, each of us in order, freely and plainly the true state of our souls . . ."[3] In order to assess the soul's state, Wesley developed three categories of "searching questions":

- Have you carefully abstained from doing evil?
- Have you zealously maintained good works?
- Have you constantly attended on all the ordinances of God?[4]

Having to answer such questions led to an atmosphere of spiritual authenticity and accountability, which proved beneficial to many Methodists. Thomas

Morris, a Methodist circuit rider, wrote in 1816 about his experience of class meetings: "Here where only pious friends are presumed to be present, where all would help and none would hinder us in the pursuit of spiritual life, we can freely talk over our hopes and fears, trials and deliverances, resolutions and prospects in the way to heaven."[5]

Look again at John Wesley's searching questions and Thomas Morris's description of class meetings, and you'll see that the word *soul* isn't limited to a private sphere of personal spirituality. Methodism has long embraced a relationship between acts of piety and acts of mercy, which correspond loosely to the chapters in this book: prayer and learning (piety), as well as mentoring and transformation (mercy). The goal of the Christian life for people called Methodist is sanctification: making all things holy, from the dark depths of one's soul to the structures that sustain injustice in our world. "Weaving these dimensions together," explains Randy Maddox, "Wesley urged his followers to support one another in the pursuit of *truly holistic salvation*, seeking God's gracious transformation of our lives and of our various social structures"[6] (emphasis added).

CHAPTER 1

Pray

Each moment draw from earth away my heart,
that lowly waits thy call;
speak to my inmost soul, and say,
"I am thy love, thy God, thy all!"
To feel thy power, to hear thy voice,
to taste thy love, be all my choice.
Amen.[1]
–Gerhard Tersteegen, translated by John Wesley

A PORTRAIT OF PRAYER

One of the most heartrending stories in the Bible has to do with Hannah. Unable to have children, while her husband's other wife bursts at the seams with babies, Hannah is heartbroken. Every year, the whole family heads to the shrine at Shiloh, where the other wife tortures Hannah with bumper stickers on her car (you know the ones), "I have a boatload of kids, all of them honor students at Ephraim Elementary School."

During one particular trip, Hannah gets it from all sides. The narrator of the story describes dear Hannah as sorely distressed, weeping bitterly, in misery, deeply troubled, full of anxiety and puzzlement. Such a sad day for Hannah. The other wife ridicules her. Her husband Elkanah only makes matters worse by failing to understand her shame and pain and asking, "Am I not more to you than ten sons?" (1 Samuel 1:8). And Eli, the priest at Shiloh, condemns her as a drunk because she prays fervently yet silently, like she is muttering to herself. "How long will you make a drunken spectacle of yourself?" he barks. "Put away your wine" (1:14).

The narrator of this story doesn't comment much on Hannah's grief-filled situation. Yet, as so often happens in scripture, he uses contrast for emphasis—in this case the contrast between Hannah and her son and Eli and his sons. From this contrast, we learn invaluable insights about prayer. So before you delve any further into this chapter, we recommend you put this book down and read the story of Hannah in 1 Samuel 1:1–3:21, paying careful attention to this contrast (and jotting some notes down, too).

TWO POSTURES

The story begins with "Hannah rose" and "Eli the priest was sitting" (1:9). She rose, he sat. She moves, he is idle. She is a go-getter, he is a non-starter. She takes initiative, he exudes inertia. Two very different postures, and only the first is a preface to prayer.

TWO PIETIES

Hannah prayed out of deep distress, yet Eli, the priest—the paid minister at God's sacred place—thought she was drunk. He couldn't recognize heartfelt prayer. Again, two different pieties, the one unvarnished and honest, the other defending the shrine of God from perceived improprieties, from an embarrassing display of emotion. Only the first is authentic prayer. First of all, Hannah's prayer was ongoing, untimed. After "she prayed to the LORD" (1:10) and made a vow to dedicate her son (1:11), Hannah *continued* to pray (1:12). Second, Hannah's prayer was informal—silent, private, unpretentious: "Hannah was praying silently; only her lips moved, but her voice was not heard; therefore Eli thought she was drunk" (1:13). Paul knew something of this sort of prayer, and he wrote about it to the church in Rome, "Likewise the Spirit helps us in our weakness; for we do not know how to pray as we ought, but that very Spirit intercedes with sighs too deep for words" (Romans 8:26).

TWO PIECES OF EQUIPMENT

Hannah's son had "a little robe" (1 Samuel 2:19), Eli's sons a "three-pronged fork" (2:13). Eli's sons were gluttonous and greedy. They sent a servant to stick a fork with a third prong that would get whatever meat the servant stabbed in the pot. This was against the rules for priests, which devoted only certain portions of the meat to priests (Deuteronomy 18:3; Leviticus 7:28-36). Eli's sons used it to grab the meat while the fat—God's portion, not theirs—was still on it, before it was boiled. If the cook refused, they'd say, "No, you must give it now; if not, I will take it by force" (1 Samuel 1:16).

Samuel wore a simple linen ephod, a little robe his mother made him each year and gave to him during the family's annual pilgrimage to Shiloh. Such a curious detail this is! Would she spend the time on the trip home planning the fiber and design of next year's robe? Would she use linen spun from flax plied together with wool spun from sheep? Would she add a bit of blue to signify her son's priestly service? Would she add a few inches under the arm and to the length, as she guessed the growth of her boy? Would Hannah not have prayed for her son as she spun and carded and dyed and sewed the robe for him each year? And what did Samuel think of these little robes? Was this his only remembrance of home, of family, of his mother?

Whatever Hannah thought and Samuel remembered, the robe came to represent this simple son of a prayerful mother. After Samuel had died, King Saul went to a witch and asked her to call up Samuel from the dead in order to ask for his guidance. She saw "a ghostly form . . . like an old man coming up, wrapped in a robe" (1 Samuel 28:13-14, our translation). Saul knew in an instant that this was Samuel.

There is something significant in this detail of Samuel's robe for our prayer lives. When you find it almost impossible to concentrate, when your mind wanders, your head spins, take something in your hands. Write your prayers in a journal. Knit something. Build something. Hold something—a cross, a favorite book, a symbol of faith you hold dear—and pray. And let that movement or gesture or item provide a measure of focus to your prayers.

TWO POSTURES REVISITED

Hannah's son Samuel had a vision, a threefold call from God. When he heard God's call, Samuel, so much like his mother, "ran" to Eli the first time, then he "arose and went" to Eli the second time, and, when he heard God's voice a third time, "arose and went to Eli" (3:4-8 KJV). Where was

Eli during all of this? "Lying down in his room" (3:2). And what was he doing? Telling Samuel to "lie down." Three times Eli told an anxious and eager Samuel to go back to bed; only the third time did he tell Samuel to listen (3:5-10).

Hannah and her son exhibited an earnestness in prayer that was simply lost to the professional priest Eli—and his sons, too. For Eli and his sons, prayer was a livelihood; for Hannah and her son, prayer was a lifeline.

We also learn from Samuel that prayer is not just talking *to* God. Prayer is also about *listening*. It's a rare time when God speaks directly—it was rare, too, for Samuel—but this boy was poised to hear, ready to run, eager to rise. We don't need to fill the space with talk. In fact, remember how the story of Samuel's call ends? "Speak, for your servant is listening" (3:10). Listening is just as much a part of prayer as speaking.

We have garnered a great deal from Hannah's story about prayer—soulful, soul-feeding prayer.

- A healthy posture for prayer is rising, getting up, being ready, and, in Samuel's case, rising and running. Hannah and Samuel both rose: one to speak, the other to listen.
- Prayer takes time. There are no shortcuts. Hannah prayed, then vowed, then prayed some more.
- Prayer needn't conform to a formula. Hannah dove headlong into prayer, so go ahead and just pray. Pray out loud. Pray silently. But whatever you do, *pray*.
- When you just can't pray, can't focus, can't think straight, incorporate movement: write, knit, build—and pray.
- Prayer is often about listening. So be alert and leave space to listen for God's prompts, whispers, and shouts.
- Finally, prayer involves patience. It may take more than once for God to get through to you. Samuel, as eager as he was, did not hear God the first or second time around. So be patient with yourself. If you think you've missed something, go back and listen again.

THE WHEN, WHERE, AND HOW OF PRAYER

Throughout this chapter, we'll learn about prayer from people, some familiar, others not, who prayed, and prayed well, prayed often, prayed effectively. People like Hannah, Samuel's mother, whom we met in a story buried deep in the Old Testament. People like Jesus, in the New. People like Susanna Wesley, in eighteenth-century England. People like Pandita Ramabai, who founded a mission in India in the late nineteenth century. These were praying people—strong, disciplined, devoted, praying people. We will also learn from the contemporary prayer practices of Latin American, Native American, and Korean Christians.

Whether we are seasoned people of prayer or newcomers to this practice, we will garner wonderful, practical, life-changing steps to take. It is important, though, that you don't try to take all of these steps at once. Take one or two for starters, and discover as well your own unique steps in prayer.

To help you, we'll organize this chapter around these three basic questions:

- *When to pray*
- *Where to pray*
- *How to pray*

A word of encouragement before you read further: "Practice makes perfect" doesn't apply to prayer. Prayer can't ever be perfect. It can be meaningful, wonderful, soulful—but never "perfect." It's like parenting. Once you've mastered how to raise a six-year-old boy, he turns seven. Your next six-year-old may be a very different girl, so back to the drawing board you go. In parenting, practice *never* makes perfect. But God's not interested in perfection. God is committed to formation. And just the practice—stumbling, stuttering, sometimes stultifying—of prayer forms us into God's people.

If you've ever heard a kid practice the piano or trumpet, you'll know what we mean. Squeaks and squawks and wrong notes and restarts are music to a parent's ears. Why? Simply because the kid is practicing. God wants us to practice. Wrong notes, off rhythms aren't a problem. Prayer, however and whenever, is music to God's ears. So let's get started.

WHEN TO PRAY

ANYTIME

The stories about Jesus in the Gospels tell us that he prayed anytime. At key moments of *decision*, when he needed to be resolute and ready, Jesus prayed. Immediately after his baptism and before he began his public work, Jesus spent forty days alone in the wilderness (Matthew 4:1-11). Before he selected his disciples, he "went to the mountain" and spent the entire night alone in prayer (Luke 6:12). Before his arrest, trial, and crucifixion, Jesus prayed—and prayed intensely—in the garden of Gethsemane (Matthew 26:36-46).

In the *day-to-day pressure* of ministry, Jesus prayed. After a particularly long night of work, Mark tells us, "In the morning, while it was still very dark, he got up and went out to a deserted place" (Mark 1:35).

After *success*—when adrenaline drops and public euphoria dies down—he prayed. After curing people of their diseases, Jesus "would withdraw to deserted places and pray" (Luke 5:16). After he miraculously fed the five thousand, Jesus told his disciples to leave, dismissed the crowd, and "went up the mountain by himself to pray" (Matthew 14:23). Jesus understood that success, in particular, demands withdrawal and prayer. So when his disciples returned from a successful preaching and healing mission, Jesus told them, "Come away to a deserted place all by yourselves" (Mark 6:31).

In *grief*, Jesus prayed. When he found out his cousin John had died, he "withdrew from there in a boat to a deserted place by himself" (Matthew 14:13).

Before decisions and after success, in the demands of day-to-day life, and in the throes of grief, Jesus prayed. He prayed in the morning. He prayed in the evening. And just as important, he prayed whenever there was a clear need for prayer. That clear need drove Jesus away from other people from time to time—before, after, and during the ups and downs, the peaks and troughs of an extraordinary life.

The prayers of many Native American peoples are attuned to the constancy of Jesus' prayer life. With an understanding of time as circular rather than linear, prayer becomes an untimed experience that shares the reality of eternity. Also like Jesus, many Native Americans pray throughout the night at key moments of endings and beginnings, such as a funeral or a New Year's Eve service.

MORNING

Imagine a group of women joined at dawn in prayer. Imagine that, and you understand what lay at the heart of Pandita Ramabai's Mukti Mission in Pune, India. Born into a Hindu Brahmin family, Pandita Ramabai (1858-1922) was baptized as a Christian while studying in England. She returned to India in 1889 and founded Mukti, which means "salvation," as a safe haven for young widows and orphaned girls, whom she trained, evangelized, and sent out as evangelists. She launched a daily dawn prayer meeting, which grew from seventy to five hundred women, and helped to spread the gospel message across India.

Early morning prayers constitute a staple of Korean Christianity, a practice that blossomed during the 1907 Pyongyang revival and continues to this day. Most Korean churches have early morning prayer services throughout the week at 5:00 or 6:00 a.m. These services consist of hymns, scripture readings, a brief sermon, and a lengthy time of prayer. Individuals, too, arise for early morning prayer. The first prayer of the day for Kyung Za Yim, past Women's Division president, after she sings hymns to open her heart, is "to ask God to fulfill my day with the Holy Spirit. My favorite verse is 'Don't you think the Father who conceived you in love will give the Holy Spirit when you ask him?'" (see Luke 11:13). She concludes, "Nothing can be done without prayer."

United Methodist deaconess, Fran Lynch, who lives in Alaska, explains her unique approach to morning prayer.

> I have a 15–20 minute walk to get the morning paper. This time is spent in prayer, mostly out loud so the bear and moose know that I am coming down the path and need to share their space. But I have found that there is power in speaking out loud to God with my joys, concerns and praise. To lift up loudly or to gently whisper the name of those for whom I pray more firmly places them in God's hands. Many times my prayer may be a way to

organize the task before me that day. This can help me seek God's guidance and direction.

There is something special about the morning (for those of us who don't work the night shift), before the buzz of the day begins. The thirteenth-century mystic Muslim poet, Rumi, reflects: "The breezes at dawn have secrets to tell you; don't go back to sleep." The prophet who penned some of the most spectacular and expansive strophes in all of scripture writes: "Morning by morning [God] wakens—wakens my ear to listen as those who are taught" (Isaiah 50:4).

NOON

Consider setting aside a few moments at the noon hour, or halfway through the day, for prayer. Benedictine sister, Macrina Wiederkehr, in a wonderful book, *Seven Sacred Pauses*, reminds us of the opportunity offered by this hour of illumination: "At this hour we look forward and backward, viewing about the same amount of the day. The day is half empty of its hours; the day is half full of its hours. Do we find ourselves focusing on the fact that the day is half gone or feeling delighted that much of the day is still ours with vast opportunities to use wisely?"[2]

A resource we enjoy at midday is the ten-minute service of noon prayer in the *Book of Common Prayer*. Make a copy for your wallet or purse, or find it electronically, and slip away during a pause in the day—lunch, a child's nap, a break from work—and read through it. Short as it is, this noon prayer is inspiring. What if you have almost no time during the day? Try marking midday with the simple gesture of opening your palms upward, breathing deeply, and reciting this: "God, give success to the work of my hands, give success to the work of my hands."

EVENING

Another time for prayer is at the close of the day. Why not, before you place your head on the pillow at night, set a tea candle on the nightstand alongside a brief reading for the evening? A specially selected psalm, perhaps. Or a favorite poem.

You might also experiment with an exercise of prayerful reflection called the *Daily Examen*, which is attributed to Saint Ignatius, the founder of the

Society of Jesus, or Jesuits. This prayer exercise asks you to consider two simple questions about the day:

- What was the *high* moment of the day?
- What was the *low* moment of the day?

After you have identified these moments, reflect on where God was in these moments. Then whisper a two-part prayer:

- A prayer of thanksgiving for God's accompaniment in the highs and lows of today;
- A prayer for greater wisdom tomorrow.

We've done the *Examen* with our son, who's now seventeen. Priscilla often rubs his back, asks him the two questions, and together they offer the two prayers. If you live with someone you love—an elderly parent, a spouse, children, a friend—practice the *Examen*. Chances are you are spending a few moments with them at day's end. Turn those moments into a time of reflection and prayer.

The *Examen* is simple. It's short. It's significant. It's a step in the right direction of offering the whole of your life to God.

MORNING, NOON, AND EVENING

Susanna Wesley, the mother of Methodism and nineteen children, including John and Charles, committed herself to prayer in the morning and evening and at noon. In the midst of a grueling family schedule, which included homeschooling her children six hours daily, in the midst of debts, illness, and grief (nine of Susanna's children did not live past infancy), Susanna withdrew from her brood for an hour in the morning and again in the evening and for a shorter time at noon. She advised her oldest son, Samuel,

> Examine well your heart and observe its inclinations . . . for let me tell you 'tis not a fit of devotion now and then speaks a man a Christian but 'tis a mind universally and generally disposed to all the

duties of Christianity in their proper times, places, etc. For instance, a good Christian will be cheerfully disposed to retire from the world that he may offer to his creator his sacrifice of prayer and praise. . . .[3]

It might be tempting for us to dismiss the deep piety of people from centuries past because we think life wasn't as fast-paced back then. Not true. Susanna confided in her diary that, given her choice, she would have "retired from the world" more easily, but the "hurry and distraction" of life prevented her. "Were I permitted to choose a state of life or positively to ask of God anything in this world," she wrote, "I would humbly choose and beg that I might be placed in such a station wherein I might have daily bread with moderate care without so much hurry and distraction; and that I might have more leisure to retire from the world. . . ."[4]

Susanna Wesley, in our view, offers the ideal of when to pray: *regularly*. If you don't carve out a regular time to pray, it's unlikely you'll pray very much, at least in a sustained way. Too many distractions and obligations beg for our attention. Too often The Urgent tyrannizes us, and we set aside prayer for another time that never arrives. Yet we mustn't let The Urgent, distractions, setbacks, even a fear of failure keep us from praying. So start small. Perhaps you can add one regular time each week to your prayer life.

The ideal of prayer is *regularity* more than timing. As we've seen, Jesus rose before dawn or stayed up late or prayed through the night. He prayed as he went, before decisions, after successes, in grief, and in the pulse of day-to-day life. Because he prayed so often and so intensely, his friends and followers, we'll soon see, asked him to teach them to pray. So he did. If you can't settle in to pray, start with that prayer, what Protestants call "The Lord's Prayer" and Catholics the "Our Father." If you can't even bring yourself to do that, find someone who does, someone who prays. Muster up the courage, and greet him or her with these words: "Teach me to pray."

WHERE TO PRAY

Hannah had her shrine at Shiloh. Jesus could withdraw into the wilderness or hills. Native American Christians pray at sacred places, like Bear Butte in western South Dakota. Korean Christians pray on prayer mountains—actual mountains to which they make a pilgrimage. Where do you withdraw to pray? This is a question we need to ask because, frankly, sometimes we don't pray because we have no place to pray.

Start by imagining a welcome place to which you *want* to withdraw. This needn't be complicated. For the Reverend Lusmarina Campos Garcia, it is the beach at Copacabana, Rio de Janeiro. She walks there every morning, enjoying the warmth of the sun and the azure color of the water and sky. This setting, adjacent to the forest-covered hills and the sea, evokes peacefulness and stillness.

For me (Priscilla), it is a comfortable chair in my study, which looks out to our garden. I have a table beside the chair that holds a candle and matches, a Bible, journal, and several devotional books. To make it even more cozy, the family dog usually settles into my lap while I pray.

I (Jack) had a similar chair but found myself staring at my desk, with book projects, papers to grade, e-mails to send. Far from welcoming! So I took an old chair in a corner of the bedroom, on which I threw my clothes, and turned it by ninety degrees. Now it faces the window. I have a small basket of tea candles and matches next to it, another with memo pads and pens for miscellaneous thoughts, and a shelf with a journal, a Bible, and a few devotional books. The change is stunning. What was once a record of the week's clothes is now a sacred space, a welcoming place for breathing deeply and reading slowly and praying quietly and feeling serenity. All with the turn of a chair!

Or try a windowsill. "For the years I was a single parent, in a tiny house with small children," writes Julie Barrett Ziegler, "the windowsill over my kitchen sink was my prayer altar. On the sill were a few family photos, a small votive candle, small elements from nature, a special stone from one of our daily walks, a revolving selection of postcard-sized sacred images, and a beloved saying I still use to this day, for my own strengthening: 'Fall into the Mystery placed before you—the one you will become will catch you.' I still think of that windowsill altar during challenging times and feel its empowering effect, even after all these years."[5]

So create this space. A sill. A shelf. A corner space. A closet. A prayer mat. In this space, gather prayer accoutrements. A journal. A Bible. A favorite devotional, like *The Upper Room*. A candle. A votive shrine, popular in Latin American Christianity, with objects turned into symbols of faith, such as pictures, letters, or body parts made of wax with prayers for healing, employment, resolution of a dispute, or safety for a missing relative. As Rosangela Oliveira, former United Methodist Women regional missionary in Latin America, explains, these objects represent a promise fulfilled or a blessing expected. Add some meditative music, and you are ready to rest, poised to pray. If you don't have this kind of space, put this book down, dream a little, and create it. It may not cost a penny, and it *will* change your life.

HOW TO PRAY

Before we offer some practical advice on prayer, let's return briefly to the insights we garnered on prayer from Hannah:

- Prayer involves showing up for time with God.
- Prayer involves talking to God and listening for God.
- Prayer involves following a protocol sometimes—and sometimes not.
- Prayer involves patience with yourself and with God.
- With these insights in mind and a deep breath in and out, let's look at how to pray.

STILL YOUR SOUL

This may be the toughest part of prayer—what keeps us from settling into intimacy with God in the first place. Our dear friend, a longtime United Methodist minister, talked in one sermon about the distractions that kept him from settling into a silent retreat. He had what Buddhist mystics call a "monkey mind."[6] His spiritual director at the retreat center told him he needed to "get the monkeys out of the tree." But how?

Breathe. Learning to breathe deeply—to be attentive to your own body—can be pivotal in settling into prayer. So you may want to start simply by *breathing* slowly, in and out. Imagine the breath filling a part of your body that hurts. Imagine the breath simply filling a part of your body.

Recite scripture. Then as you breathe, repeat a *favorite scripture* in concert with your breath. Try verses like these:

(Breathe in) O taste and see
(Breathe out) that the LORD is good. (Psalm 34:8)
                    Or,
(Breathe in) Be still
(Breathe out) Know that I am God! (Psalm 46:10)

Any favorite verse you can repeat time and again may help you to get the monkeys out of the tree.

Use your body. The power of breathing reminds us that the body has more of a role in prayer than we may realize. To harness your body, your breath, your mind, try this on for size. Take a prayer such as the *Gloria Patri*, and put these simple *body motions* to it, as Priscilla learned from Roy DeLeon in a workshop at St. Placid Priory in Lacey, Washington:

Glory be to the Father	raise your arms above your head
And to the Son	stretch your arms out to the sides of your body, in the shape of a cross
And to the Holy Spirit	do a slight back bend with your arms in the same position
As it was in the beginning	bend down as far as it is comfortable with your arms toward the ground
Is now	back to standing with your arms stretched out horizontally
And will be forever.	raise arms above your head
Amen.	bring your arms to prayer position in front of your chest

Repeat this comfortably as many times as it takes to loosen your body, deepen your breathing, and heighten your concentration.[7]

You can also use your body in prayer by dancing. "I believe that my deepest connection with God happens when I dance," says the Reverend

Lusmarina Campos Garcia. "I don't need to dance to a religious tune, just a tune that has the quality of making me feel I can let myself go in the hand of God and at the wind of the Spirit. And there I go. . . ."

Write. Another way to settle your soul is by writing in a journal. Make a list of everything that is on your mind. Or write in a free-form way. Whatever form you decide upon, write for yourself. Use this *journal* as a record of your *journey*, the story of your *sojourn*. Write for yourself, with an eye to years later, when you will want to return to it as you reflect upon how your life—and prayer life—has developed. Jack usually starts his prayer time with his journal in hand. It can also be helpful to end the day with a journal entry—perhaps, as one United Methodist woman told us, listing three things from that day for which you are thankful.

A journal is essential equipment for a spiritual retreat. It's like a flashlight for campers, a raincoat for backpackers, or a spatula for chefs. The journal is especially useful for getting the monkeys out of the tree at the beginning of a retreat, as one of my (Priscilla's) journal entries shows us:

> As I begin this retreat, this time away, I can already feel my pace slowing, my breath deepen. I have been fed. I have slept. And now I sit in this chapel, surrounded by quiet, gazing out onto greenery, so thankful just to be here. To be breathing . . . To be relaxing . . . I have been so far from God for so long that I don't even know how to settle myself to hear, to listen, to commune with God. But I've come expectant, joyful, ready to feel, know, see, and hear God's presence. God, speak to me through the silence, confirm your presence in life and in my life, fill me with your love, joy, and power, that I will never again live so long without communion with you. I've missed you; I long for you. Take me in your arms and rock me, fill me.

You may have your own best way to get the monkeys out of the tree. We've offered just a few strategies to settle your soul, to rest your mind—everything from repeating a simple *biblical phrase* to *breathing* in and out to using *body movements* to writing in a *journal.*

LISTEN TO GOD

When you've stilled your soul, you've put yourself in a prime place to listen to God. Silence carves out in us a particular ability to listen clearly to God.

I (Priscilla) often talk about the Holy Spirit's prompting—quiet but certain nudgings that lead us to do or say or pray something. Jack and I discuss them, spend time in common-sense discernment, and then I either act or choose not to act. I experience these "promptings" when I am listening in silence.

For most of us, however, listening to God, sitting in silence, is harder to do than talking. I (Jack) am a New Yorker, and Italian to boot, so I am more comfortable with interruptions than silence, a table with three simultaneous conversations going on than a quiet table with no conversation at all. Silence doesn't come naturally to me.

Once again, then, let's offer a model of listening—this one straight from scripture. The prophetic Book of Isaiah contains dazzling poetry, lavish visions of God's world unhindered by borders, unbounded by prejudice. The prophet who wrote these chapters saw beyond the cusp of human bias and bullying to a world in which God treasures outsiders and embraces aliens. This was not a natural vision that arose from the prophet's situation and his people's generosity. Not at all. As we'll see in Chapter Four, this prophet communicated the expansiveness of God to a people in exile, Babylonian exile imposed by powerful, merciless foreign armies. *Outsider* meant to them "oppressor." *Alien* for them meant "intruder." Yet among the outsiders is where this prophet believed salvation would take root.

To embrace a vision beyond the ordinary, to glimpse God beyond the commonplace, the prophet had to *listen*. And listen he did.

> The Lord GOD has given me
>   the tongue of a teacher,
> that I may know how to sustain
>   the weary with a word.
> Morning by morning [God] wakens—
>   wakens my ear
>   to listen as those who are taught.

The Lord God has opened my ear,
  and I was not rebellious,
  I did not turn backward. (Isaiah 50:4-5)

The servant, in this autobiographical snippet, offers a peek into the mechanics of listening—how exactly, in three clear steps, we can hear God.

- First, God arouses the servant morning by morning. Not on special holidays. Not just in church worship. *Every* day. Every *morning*. This is *routine awakening.*
- Second, the servant listens with the ear of a disciple, of an eager learner, to receive God's teaching. When the servant gets up, there is no blathering and babbling. The servant doesn't chatter. The servant listens. We don't know how. Through quiet? Through reading? However the servant learns, he is committed to *routine listening.*
- The servant's goal? Simple. To sustain the weary with a word. The servant awakens each morning to listen for a word of encouragement. What a remarkable way to start the day. This particular servant, the author of stunning prophetic poetry, knows he can't beat his hearers over the head. His hearers are exhausted by years in exile, depleted by captivity in Babylon. His hearers are worn out, and they need to become acquainted again with "the everlasting God, the Creator of the ends of the earth who does not *grow weary* or faint, whose understanding is unsearchable, who gives power to the *weary*, and strengthens the powerless. Even youths will *be weary* and faint, and the young will fall exhausted; but those who wait for the Lord shall renew their strength, they shall mount up with wings like eagles, they shall run and not faint, they shall walk and not *be weary*" (Isaiah 40:28–31, our translation, emphasis added). The people, his people, are bone weary. So he *awakens routinely*, *listens routinely*, in order to be a source of *routine encouragement.*

To develop a life of listening prayer, then, try out these three simple steps, which are rooted in the life of a visionary prophet:

- First, meet God even briefly when you wake up. Commit yourself to *routine awakening.*
- Second, listen—don't talk. Practice *routine listening.*
- Third, train for the goal of sustaining the weary with a word. Devote yourself to *routine encouragement.*

TALK TO GOD

Another "how to" for prayer is simply to talk to God. Jesus taught us to make our requests (Matthew 7:7-11). So did Paul (Philippians 4:6-7). So did Jack. I (Jack) prayed one morning about a young woman named Priscilla I'd noticed striding across campus. "God, I know I shouldn't do this," I confessed; "It's like asking for a new bike . . . but I'd really like to meet that girl." A simple request, and one I wasn't even sure I should make. A few hours later, the young woman was standing next to a mutual friend, who introduced us. My first line? "You have a beautiful smile." That's when I know God had answered my prayer, when God provided an introduction—*and an opening line.* I never would have made that one up myself! Thirty-two years later, as it turns out, that proved to be a good prayer request, after all.

Jesus' prayer. Requests are part of our relationship with God. The prayer Jesus taught his disciples, for example, is full of requests.

1. "Let your name be holy."
2. "Let your reign come."
3. "Let your will be done."
4. "Give us today our daily bread."
5. "Forgive us our sins or debts or trespasses."
6. "Lead us not into temptation."
7. "Deliver us from evil."

Still, maturity in prayer takes us beyond mere requests. Imagine a friendship where your companion talked to you only when she had needs. Not much of a relationship, is it? Notice, in fact, that the requests in Jesus' prayer take the person who prays beyond his own narrow world, past her own individual desires, to a reality full of *God's presence*, full of *forgiveness*, full of *provision*, full of *goodness*. The only request made for individual desire in this prayer is for daily bread. Survival. Basic existence. If that doesn't put our requests in perspective, we're not sure what will.

We can whittle down the seven requests in Jesus' prayer to four. We can build our prayers on these four pillars:

1. God, you are . . ." (#1 in Jesus' prayer): provide your own words of praise.
2. "Be present in our world, God" (#2-4 in Jesus' prayer): provide your own requests.
3. "Forgive me and inspire me to forgive" (#5 in Jesus' prayer): confess your own sins, as well as the names of those against whom you harbor anger and resentment.
4. "Make me good, wholly good" (#6-7 in Jesus' prayer): talk to God about where you may not be so good, those areas of your life in which you want to become more Christlike.

This is such a simple way to pray, braced by Jesus' own teaching, which offers you entrée to a world that is bigger than your own desires.

The ACTS of prayer. You can also structure how you talk to God according to the pattern called the "ACTS of Prayer." When you can't seem to get past the "request" stage of prayer, this pattern of prayer can be beneficial.

- *Adoration:* start by expressing your praise and adoration for God.
- *Confession:* continue by confessing your shortcomings and sins. You don't need to wallow in them, but you will gain perspective by listing them.
- *Thanksgiving:* thank God for provisions large and small.
- *Supplication:* make your requests known to God.

In this pattern, requests come last, once you've gained the right perspective about life. You start with who God is (adoration), continue by removing stumbling blocks in your relationship with God and others (confession), proceed with an accounting of what makes you grateful (thanksgiving) and, finally, when you are immersed in the person of God, forgiveness, and a grateful heart, you set your requests before God (supplication). By prayer's end, the requests you make may not be the same as the requests with which you started praying. Often we think of prayer as changing the course of life or prompting God to do something for us; more often prayer is a way of changing *us*.

PRAY WITH OTHERS

Pray in community. Jesus' friends asked, "Teach *us* to pray." Jesus answered in kind: "Give *us*" and "forgive *us*." We're not talking a few minutes of closing prayer at the end of a meeting. We're talking prayer with a trusted friend or family member, a small group, a congregation unbound by the time- and space-constraints of a Sunday morning church service. Praying with others can assume all kinds of creative forms.

- Praying with others can be a way to dismantle social injustices. Catalina Díaz Reyes from Chihuahua, México, relates that in Mexican border cities, which rank among the most dangerous places for women to live, prayer meetings are held in public places, from churches to city halls, to raise awareness about security issues among the women themselves as well as city governments.
- Praying with others can be combined with public action, like a protest march. The Reverend Lusmarina Campos Garcia tells the story of how she marched alongside thousands of demonstrators in the streets of Rio de Janeiro to protest a host of social injustices, from low salaries for workers to the unfair distribution of land. She recalled that, every so often, they would stop to raise their voices in a prayer of confession or the Lord's Prayer; then they continued on singing and marching.

- Praying with others can support the creation of something beautiful for someone in need, such as a prayer shawl. Knitters gather in churches across the country to knit prayer shawls for relatives whose loved ones were killed in the World Trade Center collapse, for babies born to women in prison, for Afghan refugees, for cancer patients, for women in domestic violence shelters, for nursing home residents, and for shut-ins.

- Praying with others provides a means of pouring out lament, confession, and deep suffering to God. Korean Christians embrace a form of prayer, known as *Tong-sung ki-do*, in which people pray together aloud about a situation of great need or suffering. Some describe this very active, loud form of prayer as having "the character of a visceral struggle with God. [It] is an embodied prayer. The kneeling, rocking back and forth, hands moving up and down, voices rising, and hitting the ground with a fist are all body movements that accompany prayer."[8] People shout "*Jooyeo*" (Lord) three times, then pray loudly together, crying or shouting to express collective suffering and grief, as the accompanying music gets noisier and faster. After a bit, the prayers and the music quiet down. As Myungrae Kim Lee explains about this form of prayer, "*Tong-sung ki-do* gives us healing, energy, and new hope in life for individuals and community."

READY TO PRAY

We've given you models of people who knew *when* to pray: Hannah, Jesus, Susanna Wesley, and Pandita Ramabai. We've encouraged you to create a welcoming place of *where* to pray. You can make do with just about any place, from a windowsill to a bookshelf, from a chair to a corner of a room. Just add a candle, journal, and Bible nearby. Create a place that welcomes you, that calls you to settle in for a few moments of peace and prayerful quiet. We've offered you some practical ideas of *how* to pray, both individually and collectively.

We hope you see that the steps of prayer aren't that hard. You simply have to take them. Morning or night—it doesn't matter. Before decisions or after successes—both times are fine. In the course of life's demands—that's good, too. With others or alone—either is the right way to pray. Made up or memorized—prayer is prayer. And in grief—but you knew that, didn't you?

The result? Not a perfect prayer life because there's no such thing. More like a practiced prayer life. And, we hope, people will notice that you are a person of deep prayer and, as a consequence, pose the simple request to you, "Teach us to pray." At that moment, like Jesus, you will be able to respond, "This is how you can pray."

CHAPTER 2

Learn

I want to know one thing, the way
to heaven—how to land safe on that happy shore.
God himself has condescended to teach the way:
for this very end he came from heaven.
He hath written it down in a book.
O give me that book!![1]
–John Wesley

LEARNING AT THE BIRTH OF CHRISTIANITY

Women—undaunted and unafraid women—surrounded Jesus during the hours of his death. Women—undervalued and untrusted women—announced Jesus' resurrection during the days after his death. And women—undeterred and unapologetic women—were in the upper room during the weeks that followed Jesus' ascension. Shoulder to shoulder with the apostles and other followers of Jesus, these women prepared for whatever God had in store for them. They were ready for what we now know, looking back, were the unsettling and earthshaking events of Pentecost, which Luke describes with amazing clarity in the Book of Acts:

> When the day of Pentecost had come, they were all together in one place. And suddenly from heaven there came a sound like the rush of a violent wind, and it filled the entire house where they

were sitting. Divided tongues, as of fire, appeared among them, and a tongue rested on each of them. All of them were filled with the Holy Spirit and began to speak in other languages, as the Spirit gave them ability. (Acts 2:1-4)

These events of Pentecost mark the birth of Christianity, when the church received a full measure of God's presence—what we call the Holy Spirit—and spoke up, spoke out, spoke into vast crowds their world-changing message of Jesus Christ.

How did this small band of followers prepare for Pentecost? By taking three simple steps.

THEY WAITED

The earliest followers of Jesus could have run here and there to let everyone know that God had raised Jesus from the dead. They didn't. Why? What could have kept them from spreading this remarkable word? Nothing less than Jesus' clear command: "While staying with them, [Jesus] ordered them not to leave Jerusalem, but to wait there for the promise of the Father" (Acts 1:4-5). So Jesus' closest followers and family settled down and waited for God's promise—the gift of the Holy Spirit.

Despite how tempting it was to get up and go, to spread the word *right here, right now*, in an act of pure obedience, Jesus' friends and followers chose not to work but to wait, not to travel to and fro but to tarry, not to labor but to linger. "Then they returned to Jerusalem from the mount called Olivet," Luke writes, "which is near Jerusalem, a sabbath day's journey away. When they had entered the city, they went to the room upstairs where they were staying" (Acts 1:12-13). They were so serious about taking Jesus at his word they didn't even stay at the Mount of Olives, but walked the mile and a half or so to the old city of Jerusalem, where they waited.

THEY PRAYED

They waited, but not passively. Jesus' disciples "were constantly devoting themselves to prayer, together with certain women, including Mary the mother of Jesus, as well as his brothers" (Acts 1:14). Jesus' earliest followers prayed together. They didn't fill Jerusalem with frenetic activities, even charitable ones. If they'd been out and about, they wouldn't have prayed in so sustained a way. Life would have been too busy, too frenzied, to allow time for prayer.

THEY STUDIED

After Jesus' followers had waited and prayed, Pentecost broke loose. The house was full of a violent wind. A tongue of flame rested on each one of them. Filled with the Holy Spirit, they spoke in other languages to a crowd that gathered for the occasion. "Amazed and astonished," spectators from the crowd asked, "How is it that . . . in our own languages we hear them speaking about God's praiseworthy acts" (Acts 2:7-11, our translation).

A century of Pentecostalism, with its fiery experience of God and its breathtaking growth, may make us think that the earliest followers of Jesus spoke in tongues. That's not quite right. They spoke, Luke says, in *other* tongues. The miracle of Pentecost is that individuals in the crowd, who had assembled from all around the Mediterranean Sea, could hear and understand in their own dialects what Jesus' followers proclaimed.

What was the content of these other tongues? What could the bystanders hear in their native languages? *"God's praiseworthy acts,"* which recount God's activity—powerful acts or mighty deeds—in Israel's history. In the scriptures of the early church, what Christians call the Old Testament, the phrase, "God's praiseworthy acts," captures the vast scope of God's work in the world. Moses encouraged the Israelites to "acknowledge *God's praiseworthy acts*, God's mighty hand and God's outstretched arm" (see Deuteronomy 11:2, our translation). One of Israel's poets writes:

> Sing to [God], sing praises to [God];
>   tell of all *God's praiseworthy acts* (Psalm 105:2, our translation).

Clearly something had been going on in the upper room in the days prior to Pentecost. Jesus' followers had studied scripture—God's praiseworthy acts—in order to put the events of Jesus' life, death, and resurrection into perspective. Now, filled with the Holy Spirit, they recited those praiseworthy acts in the languages of an array of nations that surrounded the Mediterranean Sea.

Strip off the spectacular, and you'll see something going on in that upper room prior to Pentecost. With all the talk of tongues and fire and drunks at 9:00 a.m., we can miss this part. *What led up to a spectacular experience of the Holy Spirit at Pentecost was the practice of ordinary disciplines: waiting, prayer, and the study of scripture—our Old Testament. Without these, the wind wouldn't have blown, the fiery tongues wouldn't have descended, the Holy Spirit wouldn't have filled an ordinary band of believers with extraordinary abilities to communicate God's word.*

We've already seen how important prayer is to our spiritual lives. Now we begin to notice how indispensable it is to study scripture alongside prayer. As Eugene Peterson, translator of *The Message*, says, "But without exegesis [serious Bible study], spirituality gets sappy, soupy. Spirituality without exegesis becomes self-indulgent. Without disciplined exegesis spirituality develops into an idiolect in which I define all the key verbs and nouns out of my own experience. And prayer ends up limping along in sighs and stutters."[2] The first Christians understood the importance of both prayer and study. They prayed, *looking ahead*, in eager expectation of the promise of the Father (Luke 24:49). They studied, *looking back*, in an earnest effort to understand Jesus in light of the Old Testament. When that promise became reality, their prayers answered, what rolled off their tongues? The praiseworthy acts of God—what they had studied intensely together.

LEARNING AS OUR FIRST PRIORITY

Serious learning did not die out after Pentecost. Sustained study did not shrink and shrivel in the presence of the drama of fiery tongues and rushing winds. On the contrary, the apostles taught, the church learned. In the aftermath of Pentecost, Luke tells us, "They devoted themselves to the apostles' teaching and fellowship, to the breaking of bread and the prayers" (Acts 2:42). They learned, first and foremost. They prayed, too. They ate together, as well, probably in imitation of Jesus' last meal, when he broke bread in the upper room. And all of this together birthed uncommon unity.

The power of learning continued well beyond Jerusalem and the earliest church that gathered there. In Antioch, a city in present-day Syria many miles to the north of Jerusalem, we see the force of learning.[3] Here's how the story goes. Believers who were persecuted in Jerusalem scattered. Some headed north to Antioch, where they spoke not only to Hebrew speakers but to Greek speakers as well. Numbers ballooned, so the church in Jerusalem sent Barnabas to Antioch. He encouraged them to be faithful and devoted, and even more people came to faith (Acts 8:1-3; 11:19-24). The next step seems an obvious one. He held a potluck lunch for new members. No, that can't be right. He held elections to fill new committee slots. No, that can't be correct either. He built a food pantry? Nope, not even that. What did Barnabas do?

He did this: after "a great many people were brought to the Lord," Luke tells us, "Barnabas went to Tarsus to look for Saul, and when he had found him, he brought him to Antioch. So it was that for an entire year they met with the church and taught a great many people" (Acts 11:24-26). What is the absolutely, no-holds-barred, first step Barnabas took when the church began to explode in numbers? He went and got an exceptional teacher, someone trained by the Pharisees, someone with intimate knowledge of scripture—the Old Testament, in this case—and brought him alongside so that together the two of them could teach the church. And for how long? A year! An entire year!

Before organized mission began. Before committees were formed. Before churches were built. Before pastors were appointed. Before any of this, Barnabas recognized that the church needed to learn. *Intensely and for a long time*. And the result?

Followers of Jesus were first called Christians in Antioch. You can almost see the cause-effect between intensive learning and Christian identity, can't you, in the way Luke tells the story? "So it was that for an entire year they met with the church and taught a great many people, and it was in Antioch that the disciples were first called 'Christians'" (Acts 11:26).

This is spectacularly important. Why did people realize these people were Christians? Because they attended weekly church services? Not exactly. Because they were active in charity? Not quite. Because all sorts of miracles occurred wherever they lived and worked? No, not even that. The realization that Christians were "Christian," Christ-people, emerged during a yearlong study of scripture.

Such rigorous devotion to learning explains why Korean Christians follow the regular practice of reading the entire Bible, from Genesis to Revelation, in a year. According to Grace Han, "Most Korean Christians know the drill: reading three to five chapters a day, you finish reading the Bible in a year. Many of them memorize their favorite verses or many of the Psalms . . . I had about 60 verses that I had to memorize when I joined the Navigator Bible study at the age of 16 in Korea. I still remember many of them." She goes on to explain that many older Koreans write out the Bible passages by hand as a "way of reading the Bible, meditation, and getting closer to the Bible."

What should the church's priority be? To learn. To study. Before we build, move, serve, plant, we must *learn*. And learning from a Bible that was written in three ancient languages—Hebrew, Aramaic, and Greek—thousands of years ago about people, including Jesus, who inhabited different cultures from ours is no small task.

Whatever the cost, the work is worth it because the product is immeasurable: knowing Jesus in a rich, deep, personal way that spreads its roots throughout scripture. Barnabas knew this. The earliest believers in Jerusalem knew this. The church in Antioch knew this. And we know this, too: the church, at its core, is a gathering of people united by a thirst for Jesus. So first things first: *learn about Jesus*. This knowledge is a storehouse, this wisdom the fountainhead of all that Christians do. Generosity, mission, diversity, and grace follow from this informed, intelligent, and intimate knowledge of Jesus. All of these characterized the church in Antioch—but they flowed from a primary commitment to learning, from a love of study, from a relentless will to know Jesus Christ.

This dedication to study and action, learning and leading, is the heart and soul of historic Methodism. Methodist luminary Lucy Rider Meyer (1849-1922), for instance, understood this relationship between scripture and sanctification, both personal and social. Meyer was a standout by all counts: a prominent lay leader in the Methodist church and a pioneer of the Methodist deaconess movement. Today United Methodist deaconesses—home missioners as well—are part of United Methodist Women. This legacy extends back more than a century to the founding of the Woman's Home Missionary Society (WHMS) of the Methodist Episcopal Church, formed in 1880. The WHMS lobbied for a deaconess movement within the church, which, by vote of the General Conference in 1888, was approved. Lucy Rider Meyer was part of these great movements and initiatives.

Early in her adult life, as a staff member for the Illinois State Sunday School Association, Meyer traveled for several years throughout the state to churches, church conventions, and Sunday school gatherings, where she found herself dumbfounded by how ignorant people in churches were of the Bible. "I became greatly impressed," she confided, "with the astonishing, and to me alarming ignorance of the Bible on the part of our Church people, Sunday-school teachers, and Christian workers. My own knowledge of the word of God was superficial enough, but when I saw people looking for Jude in the Old Testament, or for one of the minor prophets in the New, I realized the great need of more thorough and comprehensive Bible study on the part of those who were, or might become religious teachers."[4]

Meyer went on to found the first Methodist deaconess training school, the Chicago Training School for City, Home and Foreign Missions, to which she added within a few years the Chicago Deaconess Home. For over thirty years, she was its primary fundraiser, Bible teacher, and principal, while her husband, Josiah Shelley Meyer, worked alongside her as its business agent. By the time they retired, no less than forty agencies—hospitals, orphanages, training schools, and homes for the elderly—could trace their existence to the work of Lucy Rider and Josiah Shelley Meyer and graduates of the Chicago Training School.[5]

Meyer ensured that daily Bible study proved indispensable to the education deaconesses received. At the Chicago Training School, for at least an hour every morning, five days a week, deaconesses-in-training studied both the content and context of all sixty-six books of the Bible. They learned as well how to develop Bible lessons that included maps, charts, and simple drawings intended to reinforce lessons.

Meyer and her staff also ensured that study of the Bible did not produce knowledge for knowledge's sake, which could lead to a sense of scriptural superiority. Biblical knowledge for Meyer was practical knowledge. During the afternoons, therefore, deaconesses-in-training took the Bible with them as they visited house-to-house in city neighborhoods. Bible in hand, they tended the sick, impoverished, addicted, and dying. The impact of this commitment to the connection between Bible study and practical service is staggering. In one year alone, 1887-88, deaconesses-in-training paid more than five thousand visits to homes—and incorporated Bible readings and prayer in close to six hundred homes. Even more staggering is this: deaconesses-in-training taught over nineteen thousand Bible lessons in Sunday schools and more than eight thousand in industrial schools, all in a single year.[6]

Current United Methodist deaconesses continue this tradition, exemplified by Lucy Rider Meyer, in which Bible study and practical work strengthen the effectiveness of each other. As deaconess Kandi Mount explains, "We have a sterling example before us of Lucy Rider Meyer. She incorporated biblical knowledge for use as practical knowledge. I, too, find that a fine way to work and to live." Working in eight different cities in Arkansas affords Mount, a hospital chaplain, plenty of time to pray and reflect on scripture while driving. She begins her prayers for the day by quoting Psalm 19:14: "Let the words of my mouth, and the meditation of my heart / be acceptable in thy sight, / O LORD, my strength and my redeemer" (KJV). Her reliance on scripture to evoke an awareness of God's presence steels her for the work ahead: "I am completely open to the process that God will be supplying all that is needed for his children that day. Before asking my patients to trust, I trust. There is a solemnity in releasing my spirit to allow this 'free fall' into oneness with the Holy Spirit. . . . Thank you, God, for your tenderness."

Bible study informs and infuses with meaning the practical work for which deaconesses are renowned. Deaconess and research chemotherapy registered nurse, Juliet Hahn Choi, quotes scripture to help patients focus in a way "that allows them to receive their treatment as best they can with faith, trust in God. They seek peace, comfort, and refuge at a time when fear of death is so real." Mount expresses similar sentiments about the importance of talking about scripture with patients.

> Many terminal or actively dying patients vocalize fears that they
> will not reach heaven, even though they have earnestly asked
> for forgiveness. The scripture that seems to resonate with these

patients spiritually is Romans 8:38-39: "For I am persuaded, that neither death, nor life, nor angels, nor principalities, nor powers, nor things present, nor things to come, nor height, nor depth, nor any other creature, shall be able to separate us from the love of God, which is in Christ Jesus our Lord" [KJV]. I then ask these questions: "Do you have any idea how much Christ adores you? Can the blood of the cross show you the power and commitment of God's love for you? Whether you choose to accept it or not, you are God's child."

United Methodist deaconesses continue, more than 125 years after Lucy Rider Meyer began her work in Chicago, to combine Bible study with, as Mount so deftly puts it, "bringing hope and peace to the wounded, sick, and dying, physically or spiritually, in this world, that's pretty much all of us at one time or another."

LEARNING JESUS FROM THE GOSPELS

We discover in the early church and its legacy—movements like the deaconesses—an intense commitment to making Jesus known. When Peter, in the Book of Acts, encounters faithful Gentiles, non-Jews, he says this: "You know the message he sent to the people of Israel, preaching peace by Jesus Christ— he is Lord of all" (Acts 10:36). There you have it: a nice, tidy summary of the Christian faith. Yet Peter continues with a few more details, which sound like an early Christian confession of faith, a summary that early believers could memorize and bring out whenever occasion arose (which it did often in those first, feverish days of witness):

> . . . how God anointed Jesus of Nazareth with the Holy Spirit and
> with power;
> how he went about doing good and healing all who were oppressed
> by the devil, for God was with him.
> We are witnesses to all that he did both in Judea and in Jerusalem.

They put him to death by hanging him on a tree;
but God raised him on the third day and allowed him to appear,
   not to all the people but to us who were chosen by God as
   witnesses,
   and who ate and drank with him after he rose from the dead.
He commanded us to preach to the people and to testify
   that he is the one ordained by God as judge of the living and
   the dead.
All the prophets testify about him that everyone who believes in
him receives forgiveness of sins through his name. (Acts 10:38-43)

Glance even briefly at this snippet of a sermon, and you'll notice that the message of the early church was not about self-fulfillment, finding meaning in life, discovering joy in the midst of sadness. The earliest preachers and teachers told others the story of Jesus and drew people into that story.

Let's put it another way. Early Christian teaching was not particularly hearers-centered. It was *Jesus*-centered. Teachers didn't tell the story to meet hearers' needs so much as to bring hearers into the scope of Jesus' story. The question this realization raises for us is this: How can *we* learn the story of Jesus?

We can't answer this question completely, but we do want to suggest some practical strategies for scripture study, and we'll end with ways to unite study and contemplation, learning and prayer, which you can combine with the insights and strategies we offered in Chapter 1 on prayer. We want to give you something to sink your teeth into because, at the end of the day, you are people called "Christians," people called to serve your neighborhoods, towns, and cities with a vigor that is fed by a steady stream of study and a deep dedication to wisdom.

STUDY EACH GOSPEL

Whenever you engage in Bible study, take a moment to pray beforehand this collect from the *Book of Common Prayer* that John Wesley commended for himself and his followers: "Blessed Lord, who hast caused all holy Scriptures to be written for our learning, grant that we may in such wise hear them, read, mark, learn, and inwardly digest them, that by patience, and comfort of thy holy Word, we may embrace, and ever hold fast, the blessed hope of everlasting life which thou has given us in our Saviour Jesus Christ."[7]

A place to begin your study is with the Gospels—Matthew, Mark, Luke, and John. The church chose—wisely, it seems—to preserve four versions of the story of Jesus rather than only one. Each Gospel has its own emphasis:

- Matthew is concerned to show that Jesus' teaching was in line with the Judaism in which Jesus was reared; Jesus was not a novelty but someone who fulfilled the heart and soul of the Jewish scriptures.
- Mark underscores the need for intense, self-denying commitment to Jesus; Jesus calls his flawed followers to this level of discipleship although, for the most part, they aren't up to the task of following him to and through the cross.
- Luke is keen to demonstrate that Jesus is on the side of the marginalized and the poor—economically poor—as well as ethnic outsiders and women. For instance, Luke's Gospel brings out stories Jesus tells of Samaritans—those "half-brothers and sisters" whom many Jews despised.
- John places Jesus within the great categories of Greek philosophy as well as the rhythm of Jewish feasts; Jesus is the eternal *logos*, the unifying principle of the universe, as well as a teacher who calls himself the "light of the world" during Hanukkah, the Jewish Feast of Lights.

Take time to read through the Gospels one at a time. It doesn't really matter which order you choose because each provides its own unique testimony to Jesus. Keep a journal of your thoughts as you read, charting your impression of Jesus as you study each Gospel. Keep a journal also of questions that this reading raises; Jesus is not always as benign or friendly as we may expect. Turn your questions into prayers, your reflections into starting-points for meditation. Come to think of it, you may want to keep a separate small notebook for each Gospel, four records of your reading.

COMPARE THE GOSPELS WITH ONE ANOTHER

When I (Jack) returned from college to my home on Long Island, I decided to offer a Bible study for anyone who was interested. A motley crew collected in my parents' living room once a week, and the lively conversation centered around study of the Gospels, but not one at a time. Too often reading one book at a time—in this case, one Gospel at a time—leads, if we are honest, to boredom because we don't know what we're looking for.

If that has ever happened to you, then try this method. Compare the first three Gospels—Matthew, Mark, and Luke—which are called the *Synoptic Gospels* because they look (optic) together (syn—as in sym-phony) at Jesus. They actually share a lot of material, and it looks to most people who've spent their lives studying the Gospels that one was the source of the others. Let's put it this way:

- Mark was probably the earliest Gospel; most of Mark you can also find in Matthew and Luke, though with slight changes and in a different order.
- Matthew and Luke also share teachings of Jesus they didn't get from Mark. The Gospels of Matthew and Luke contain sayings, in other words, that aren't in Mark. For instance, you'll find the Lord's Prayer or Our Father, which we glanced at in Chapter 1, in Matthew and Luke but not Mark. The same with the Beatitudes ("Blessed are . . ."). And lots of other sayings.
- Sometimes Matthew has material that no one else has. The same for Luke. (Check out the first two chapters of each Gospel—the stories of Jesus' birth and early childhood—and you'll find material that no other Gospel has.)

Here's what you can do to help you study the Synoptic Gospels as you learn Jesus:

Buy a set of synoptic parallels.[8] This resource sets in columns any stories and sayings that occur in more than one Gospel. Or, though it's a little trickier, you can make your own synoptic parallels if you have a computer that can create charts and tables. Find a story or saying in one Gospel, and look for the same story or saying in the others. Just the typing of texts into these columns is a good discipline, an exercise that calls your attention to stories and sayings you might otherwise read too quickly.

Once you've organized a Gospel story or saying into columns, get some colored pencils or highlighters. (This can easily be done on a computer. For those uncomfortable with computers, colored pencils and paper will do.) Do this:

- Whenever two or three Gospels (depending upon how many columns you've filled) have exactly the same wording, underline or highlight them in blue (or whatever color you prefer).
- Whenever Matthew makes a change in Mark's Gospel (remember, Mark was probably the earliest Gospel), underline or highlight that change in another color, let's say green. (You could actually use more than one color here: one for additions, another for omissions, still another for modifications).
- Whenever Luke makes a change in Mark's Gospel, underline or highlight that change in another color, let's say red.
- Whenever Matthew and Luke—but not Mark—have sayings in common, highlight the differences in still another color. How about purple?

This may sound tedious, but it's really fun, practical, and fascinating—a terrific way to learn the story of Jesus.

This way of reading the Gospels in comparison with one another has several benefits. First, reading this way can help you appreciate the material that the early church prized, stories and sayings that occur in all three Gospels. Second, reading this way helps us learn Jesus by discovering the unique portraits the church preserved in each separate Gospel. Third, this way of reading keeps us paying attention. Who doesn't like colors? And fourth, this way of reading keeps us asking questions, and who doesn't like puzzles? When you see a change, ask yourself (or others in your group), "Why?" Why did Matthew change this story in Mark's Gospel? Why do Matthew and Luke preserve these sayings in such different ways?

To prime the pump, let's look together at a couple of examples:

Example #1: Before he went public, Jesus traveled to the Jordan River to be baptized by his cousin John. Here's how the story goes in three columns:

Matthew	Mark	Luke
3:13 Then Jesus came from Galilee to John at the Jordan, to be baptized by him.	1:9 In those days Jesus came from Nazareth of Galilee and was baptized by John in the Jordan.	
14 John would have prevented him, saying, "I need to be baptized by you, and do you come to me?" 15 But Jesus answered him, "Let it be so now; for it is proper for us in this way to fulfill all righteousness." Then he consented.		
16 And when Jesus had been baptized,		3:21 Now when all the people were baptized, and when Jesus also had been baptized and was praying,
just as he came up from the water,	10 And just as he was coming up out of the water,	
suddenly the heavens were opened to him	he saw the heavens torn apart	the heaven was opened,
and he saw the Spirit of God descending	and the Spirit descending	22 and the Holy Spirit descended upon him in bodily form
like a dove and alighting on him.	like a dove on him.	like a dove.
17 And a voice from heaven said, "This is my Son, the Beloved, with whom I am well pleased."	11 And a voice came from heaven, "You are my Son, the Beloved; with you I am well pleased."	And a voice came from heaven, "You are my Son, the Beloved; with you I am well pleased."

Pay attention, read slowly, and you'll notice a few details you might overlook if you read one Gospel at a time. First, once you've set your columns and colored them in, you'll notice that Matthew goes to great lengths to show that Jesus was fulfilling all righteousness when he was baptized. What's behind this addition to Mark's story? Just this: John preached a baptism of repentance, of change, which implies that people who are baptized have done something wrong. Matthew eliminates this implication by changing the reason for Jesus' baptism from repentance to fulfilling God's righteousness. This change, therefore, raises some real questions, questions you can reflect upon, meditate upon, talk to others about, such as, "Why wasn't Mark bothered by this?" and "Why was Matthew so bothered that he included this conversation between John the Baptist and Jesus?"

Second, notice that in Mark's Gospel, this is a private scene between God and Jesus. No one else sees the dove or hears the divine words. In Luke's Gospel, this happens when others are baptized, too ("when all the people were baptized"). Again, by getting your columns straight and your colored pencils to work, you'll notice that, in Luke's Gospel, this isn't a private scene but a public vision. Ask yourself why. Why does Luke present the dove and heavenly voice as a public event? (The same, you'll see, for Matthew, too.) Write your thoughts in your journal. Ask others what they think. Be curious. Try to understand the story of Jesus.

Example #2: Matthew and Luke present different versions of the Lord's Prayer.

Matthew	Luke
6:7 "When you are praying, do not heap up empty phrases as the Gentiles do; for they think that they will be heard because of their many words. 8 Do not be like them, for your Father knows what you need before you ask him.	11:1 He was praying in a certain place, and after he had finished, one of his disciples said to him, "Lord, teach us to pray, as John taught his disciples."
9 Pray then in this way:	2 He said to them, "When you pray, say:

Our Father in heaven, hallowed be your name.	Father, hallowed be your name.
10 Your kingdom come. Your will be done, on earth as it is in heaven.	Your kingdom come.
11 Give us this day our daily bread.	3 Give us each day our daily bread.

12 And forgive us our debts,
    as we also have forgiven our
    debtors.
	4 And forgive us our sins,
	    for we ourselves forgive everyone
	    indebted to us.

13 And do not bring us to the time
    of trial,
    but rescue us from the evil one.
	And do not bring us to the time of
	trial."

14 For if you forgive others their trespasses, your heavenly Father will also forgive you; 15 but if you do not forgive others, neither will your Father forgive your trespasses."	5 And he said to them, "Suppose one of you has a friend, and you go to him at midnight and say to him, 'Friend, lend me three loaves of bread; 6 for a friend of mine has arrived, and I have nothing to set before him.' 7 And he answers from within, 'Do not bother me; the door has already been locked, and my children are with me in bed; I cannot get up and give you anything.' 8 I tell you, even though he will not get up and give him anything because he is his friend, at least because of his persistence he will get up and give him whatever he needs."

These two versions of the same prayer have a lot in common, but some significant differences, too. First, it's clear from the start that Matthew and Luke set the Lord's Prayer in different contexts. In Matthew's Gospel, the prayer occurs in the Sermon on the Mount; in Luke's Gospel, Jesus offers this prayer after he himself has withdrawn to pray. Second, there are a lot of small differences between these versions. That's not hard to explain. This prayer was probably used throughout the early church in a variety of places around the Mediterranean Sea. When sayings and stories circulate orally, they often undergo an array of minor changes. That's probably what happened here. And third, Matthew and Luke present different purposes for this prayer. Look at what follows the prayer itself. For Matthew, the main point is forgiveness; for Luke, the main point is persistence in prayer. These don't contradict each other; they simply draw different reasons for Jesus' teaching.

This may seem like a crash course in seminary. In fact, these are nothing more or less than two ways of reading the Gospels that focus your attention on Jesus, minimize distractions, and make you active rather than passive readers. In a sense, they help you read *slowly*. Be curious, and, at those points where something in the Gospels piques your interest, pause and meditate, reflecting upon this part of the story. And, as always, jot your thoughts down in a journal, to which you can return time and again as you learn Jesus for the rest of your life.

LEARNING JESUS IN CONFERENCE WITH OTHERS

John Wesley commended his followers to read the Bible in conference with others; in other words, he promoted a communal approach to complement one's personal study. He expected that regular participation in class would form Christian disciples devoted to reading the Bible and putting into practice its central precepts. Such people would be beneficial companions with whom to study the Bible.

He also recommended that reading the Bible in conference with others should be marked by "a spirit of openness to dialogue," according to Wesleyan scholar, Randy Maddox. How can we cultivate a spirit of openness to dialogue? By discussing the Bible with those who hold different interpretations from our own, by reading the Bible alongside them. Wesley himself invited any who "believed that he presented mistaken readings of the Bible in his *Sermons* to be in touch, so that they could confer together over Scripture."[9] What a picture! Imagine what this approach to Bible study might initiate for congregations—whole denominations, too—which are presently terribly divided over a host of issues, including homosexuality, abortion, immigration, and gun control.

Learning in conference with others can also include engaging with biblical interpreters from around the globe. Diverse vantage points from an array of contexts open fresh ways of reading the biblical text. To see how this works in practice, let's explore two interpretations of Matthew 5–7, the Sermon on the Mount, chapters that Wesley described as "the noblest compendium of religion found in the oracles of God."[10]

Kenyan Hannah Kinoti focuses her interpretation of the Sermon on the Mount on the Beatitude, "Blessed are the merciful" (Matthew 5:7). The practice of mercy, Kinoti suggests, "demands action to alleviate all types of suffering—physical, spiritual, and that which arises from structural injustices." To illustrate her point, Kinoti tells the story of a Kenyan woman named Mrs. Mutahi.

> Mrs. Mutahi, who lived in the poorer part of Nairobi with her family, had some friends over for a lunch party. When her guests left, she got busy clearing dishes and throwing the rubbish in the common rubbish bin outside. Later in the evening, she went to throw away some more rubbish and was surprised to find a group of boys hanging on the rubbish bin and picking clean the chicken bones she had thrown away earlier. She invited the boys into the house and gave them the leftovers from the lunch. The boys had no homes to return to, so that night they slept on the floor of the small house. On the following several evenings, the boys kept returning in greater numbers until the house proved too small for them. Her daughter who did some tailoring in the city centre offered to take the boys some bread for lunch at a public park in the city. That worked well, but the boys still turned up at the house in the evenings. The lunches were also sometimes rudely interrupted by civic authorities who dispersed the "parking boys," whom they considered a menace.
>
> Eventually Mrs. Mutahi proposed to her "family" of street urchins, which by now included girls, that they should all move to

the foot of the Ngong hills, on the outskirts of Nairobi, where she and her husband owned a small plot of land. There they could all construct a much bigger house than the present quarters. Some of the children deserted her because they preferred the dazzle of the city centre, but some twenty children moved with her.

I visited Ngong Hills Children's Home with a group of women from my church, and the stories this woman told moved us to tears. One was how she "hijacked" an eight-year-old-girl from a commune of street boys. The girl needed immediate medical attention due to damage caused by sexual assaults in the commune. In one busy hospital, she only got rebukes for "neglecting your daughter and coming to us too late to do impossible repairs." In another hospital, treatment was forthcoming, but the hospital bill was prohibitive. Overwhelmed and deeply moved by the needs of her new family, this woman of faith resorted to prayer for specifics, and God intervened in numerous instances. The children were wonderful and impressed us by their good manners and spiritual awakening.[11]

Another interpretation of Matthew 5–7 comes from the Philippines. Helen Graham, a Maryknoll sister in the Philippines, focuses upon the beatitude, "Blessed are the peacemakers" (Matthew 5:9). Graham interprets peacemaking from a Philippine context. She describes the efforts of peace advocates to set up peace zones in the Philippines.

One of the first peace zones was established, in the face of severe tension, in a small village in the southern part of the island of Negros called Cantomanyog. The plan started by forming a "Peace Caravan" to encircle the island, stopping at major cities along the way and ending at the little mountan village of Cantomanyog, where a peace zone was to be set up. The caravan set off for its five-day tour around the island. As it was approaching Cantomanyog, Bishop Fortich and several priests began to prepare for a eucharistic celebration to be held upon the caravan's arrival.

Graham describes how about a mile or so from Cantomanyog, a group of soldiers with M16 assault rifles disembarked from a military helicopter gunship and set up a blockade. When the peace caravan arrived, they saw the armed soldiers. But that wasn't all. Behind the soldiers, they also saw "a small table prepared for liturgy." Despite the tension, the priests began the Eucharistic liturgy.

> By the time of the liturgy's kiss of peace, the people from Cantomanyog who had been blocked by the barricade had braved their way through and had slipped into the crowd at the liturgy. Amidst many tears, and with the remaining people at the barricade and the heavily armed soldiers with guns pointed, the setting up of the first peace zone in Negros was announced over a loudspeaker by a young woman from Cantomanyog, who was holding a small child in her arms.[12]

Peacemaking, in this Philippine context, is powerful. Peacemaking is personal. Peacemaking is political.

Imagine studying the Beatitudes in this way. You begin, first, by setting the versions of Matthew's and Luke's Gospels side by side.

Second, you grab a fistful of colored pencils and highlight similarities and differences. There are important ones, such as the beatitude that reads "Blessed are the poor in spirit" in Matthew (5:3) and "Blessed are you who are poor" in Luke (6:20). Lots to ponder in just this difference.

Third, read the Beatitudes in conference with global partners—a way of reading that lets you see how a Kenyan woman embodies the beatitude, "Blessed are the merciful," by gathering up orphans, and how Philippine activists live out the beatitude, "Blessed are the peacemakers," by courageously celebrating the Eucharist or Lord's Supper in the shadow of military might. Both readings are different—*very* different. Yet both bring to light elements of Jesus' teaching we might overlook if we read only in conference with those who think like us. These interpretations challenge us with an authentic and active Jesus, whose peacemaking and mercy led him into direct conflict with anyone who preferred the superficial peace of the status quo; Jesus unmasked attempts at peacekeeping that came at the expense of the poor.

Fourth, through serious study and lively conversation, enter with Jesus into the fray of life. Bible study must always be practical, as among deaconesses, always applicable to how we live, always producing in us, not only a spirit of openness to dialogue, but also a spirit of openness to action.

LEARNING JESUS THROUGH *LECTIO DIVINA*

Another way to learn Jesus is by reading scripture in a slow, attentive, and meditative way. Eugene Peterson perfectly expresses the purpose of spiritual reading when he writes that a rich and slow study of scripture

> is an act of love. . . . Exegesis [serious study] is loving God enough to stop and listen carefully to what he says. It follows that we bring the leisure and attentiveness of lovers to this text, cherishing every comma and semicolon, relishing the oddness of this preposition, delighting in the surprising placement of this noun. Lovers don't take a quick look, get a "message" or a "meaning," and then run off and talk endlessly with their friends about how they feel.[13]

Why do we need to read so slowly? Peterson helps us again by comparing the biblical world with ours:

> The Bible is deep and wide with God's love and grace, brimming over with surprises of mercy and mystery, peppered with alarming exposés of sin and bulletins of judgment. This is an immense world, and it takes time to adjust to the majesty—we're not used to anything on this scale. We've grown up on the streets and back alleys of Lilliput—it takes a while for our eyes to adjust. If we move into the Scriptures too fast or move through them too fast, we'll miss most of what is here.[14]

Lectio divina, a Latin phrase that means "holy or sacred reading," involves a slow, contemplative praying of the scriptures. *Lectio* developed in monasteries where the monks read scripture communally in the liturgy as many as seven times throughout the day and night. This practice encouraged the memorization of scripture at a time when literacy was low and the cost of books high. In the early sixth century, Saint Benedict, founder of the Benedictine order, lifted up *lectio* as a principal activity in the daily life of a monk that should consume approximately three hours a day and even more on Sunday.[15]

Boiled down to its essence, *lectio divina* is listening for the voice of God—which takes us back, of course, to getting those monkeys out of the tree. Saint Benedict expressed the purpose of *lectio* in the opening sentences of his *Rule*: "Listen with the ear of your heart."[16] Psalm 40:6, which says literally, "You have cut for me ears," offers a powerful image of spiritual reading. The psalmist "was bold to imagine God swinging a pickax, digging ears in our granite blockheads so that we can hear, really hear, what he speaks to us."[17] Deep listening enables us, with practice, to silence all the other voices that compete for attention and to foster a "posture of receptivity to God. . . . Through lectio, a friendship with the Holy One develops and a new way of life is born."[18]

Lectio divina can be done both individually and collectively. I (Priscilla) was initially introduced to communal *lectio divina* through the Benedictine sisters at St. Placid Priory in Lacey, Washington. I gather with other Associates of the Priory monthly to engage in this collective practice. Both of us use *lectio divina* in our classes at Seattle Pacific University. Students treasure this time. Again and again, they say how much they look forward to the quiet during the buzz of their college days.

In order to get your feet wet with this practice, turn back for a moment to the practicalities of our chapter on prayer. You'll cherish *lectio divina* if you are in a quiet space—the prayer place you've created for yourself—and have enough time, at least twenty minutes, so you don't have to rush. A regular time, of course, is optimal, just as a regular time for meals and exercise and sleep is best, too. You may want to establish a ritual that marks a transition into *lectio divina*: lighting a candle, singing slowly a verse from a favorite hymn, or any number of the settling methods we suggested in Chapter 1. Continue by selecting a few lines from the Bible or a devotional book—the briefer, the better—for the day. After breathing and settling yourself, read the scripture text three times.

- The first time, listen for a *word* that summons your attention. Take about a minute in silence to mull the word over and wonder why this word struck you.
- Second time around, listen for an *emotion* the saying or story stirs. Take about two minutes in silence this time to wonder why you felt this way. Does the word evoke a memory or an association, perhaps? Is God speaking to you—taking a pickax to your ears—through this emotion?
- The third time, listen for an *invitation* for the near future—the coming hours and days ahead. Mull this over in silence for three minutes. This invitation may be strikingly simple. It may be an occasion to express joy and gratitude, to mourn a loss, to confess, to mark an intention to follow through on an action—or anything else you hear God calling you to in the silence.

If you're in a group setting, take turns after each time of silence to share aloud first the *word*, then the *emotion*, and finally the *invitation*. If you're on your own, you may want to jot down in your journal the word you are struck by, the emotion you feel, and the invitation you hear.

Once you've completed these steps, be still a few minutes longer and allow the *lectio* to continue to form you. Don't leave the stillness, the quiet, the composure, too quickly. Then, when you are ready or the demands of life creep up, close out the *lectio* with the Lord's Prayer, the *Gloria Patri*, or a benediction.

An example of lectio divina: Let's stay with learning Jesus from the Gospels. Imagine you've selected Mark 14:7, "For you always have the poor with you, and you can show kindness to them whenever you wish; but you will not always have me."

- The first time around, any number of *words* might grab your attention: poor, kindness, whenever, always, me. You're now bringing the "attentiveness of lovers to this text, cherishing every comma and semicolon, relishing the oddness of this preposition, delighting in the surprising placement of this noun." Whichever it is, wonder at the word that attracts your attention.

- The *emotion* evoked by the second reading might be guilt at what you don't do for the poor, yearning to cultivate kindness, or even gratitude that a woman understood what men didn't. However you feel, wonder at the emotion stirring in you.
- The *invitation* might be as simple as putting granola bars in your pocket to give to beggars or as complex as responding to a deep longing to break out of a routine that keeps you locked into your own economic and social class. Whatever you hear, wonder at the invitation God is extending to you.

What word you hear loudest, what emotion stirs in you the strongest, what invitation you receive the most forcefully, you are now in the presence of God, and God is taking a pickax to your ears. You are learning Jesus in the deepest regions of your will, your intellect, your heart, your body. Maybe even, by now, the monkeys have climbed down from the trees!

CHAPTER 3

Mentor

Make us faithful in all our contacts with our neighbors,
that we may be ready to do good and bear evil,
that we may be just and kind, merciful and meek,
peaceable and patient . . . that so glorifying thee here
we may be glorified with thee in thy heavenly kingdom.[1]
–John Wesley

When I (Jack) was five years old, I headed to kindergarten, where I played with wooden toy trucks and kickballs. About that time, my mother's much-loved Aunt Gen made the trek from Pittsburgh, Pennsylvania, to Long Island, New York, where the Levison family lived. As my mother tells the story, her Aunt Gen said to her, in no uncertain terms, "You need a life outside this house." My mother had been raising kids since 1950, and it was now 1961. But what to do? Aunt Gen made one more suggestion: "How about bowling?" So off my mother scooted to Mid-Island Bowl, where she signed up for "The Pajama League," which consisted primarily of mothers who bowled while their kids were in school.

In that league, she met Joan and Mary. They became friends. Friends for years to come. She invited them to a retreat at a rustic church camp in the Catskill Mountains. She invited them to join a Bible study of eight to ten women who met around her dining room table every Tuesday morning. She invited them to my sister's wedding at the church where my family worshiped, and they were struck by its simplicity and authenticity. Finally, after years of friendship and hospitality, both Mary and Joan came to faith, becoming lifelong, devoted Christians. Mary's daughter Susan did remarkable work with foster children. One of Joan's sons became a minister.

As I asked my mother over the phone recently about the women she had mentored, the stories swelled. Mary and Joan were just the tip of the iceberg. I reminded her of Lucy, and my mother laughed warmly, "Oh, Lucy was the first." Coffee, of course, and meetings called "sword clubs," where they studied the Bible. Then she recalled Doug and Helen, whom she met as an Avon Lady. A knock on *their* door led to an invitation to ours—and an evening Bible study led by my father, who had recently become a Christian. There were Sallie and John, who would drive my father home from the train station after a long day in Manhattan. My mother would invite them in for something cold to drink in the summer, something warm in the winter. This led to conversations and friendship and an invitation to church.

During the talk with my mother, three characteristics of a powerful mentor became clear. First, a mentor is *intentional* about mentoring others. My mother went out of her way to guide, teach, and lead others in the faith. Sometimes this was informal. Sometimes this took place in a regular Bible study or prayer meeting. *Always* she was on the lookout, alert, aware of people to engage in conversation about life, family, faith.

Second, mentoring others in the faith almost always took place through *hospitality*. I remember the way my mother, on Sunday mornings, would pick up children from all around the neighborhood and cram them—as many as six in the days before seatbelts—in the back of her car in order to take them to Sunday school. And I will never forget Sunday afternoons, when my parents invited people who had visited our church over for cold cuts, soda, and sour seeded rye bread, fresh and warm from the Jewish bakery. I don't ever recall having someone in our home—and there were plenty—without the offer of something to eat or drink.

Third, and most important, mentoring took place in the context of *friendship*. Mary and Joan. Lucy. Sallie and John. These were not projects. They were not just members of a class or a Bible study. They were—they still are—first and foremost friends. Sisters and daughters, brothers and sons, in the faith.

My mother wasn't trained for this. She didn't go to a Christian college or seminary. In fact, though she was salutatorian in her high school class in rural Pennsylvania, she was the step-daughter of a coal miner, so there was no money for college. She trained, not to be a minister, deaconess, or lay pastor, but a reservations agent with an airline. She was, in short, a woman with an ordinary background and an extraordinary vision for mentoring people in the faith.

THREE CIRCLES OF LEADERSHIP

While my mother had no structures in the church that made it easy or convenient for her to be a mentor, The United Methodist Church today, United Methodist Women in particular, provides precisely those places of hospitality and friendship that sets the table for a robust commitment to mentoring. United Methodist Women, in fact, occupies a unique niche for mentoring in the church. Look around, and you'll see that most groups in the church are geared toward people in different stages of life. Many committees are populated by adults. Children's ministries are for parents of little kids. Then there is the youth group and separate groups for "young singles" or "young marrieds." There are "senior Bible studies" for retirees. The church is often divided by age. Not, however, United Methodist Women, which is united not by a stage of life but by a keen commitment to Bible study and service at any age. United Methodist Women, therefore, offers an exceptional opportunity to engage in an intergenerational community of mentoring.

This chapter will be divided into concentric circles of mentoring:

- In the first section, we'll talk about being mentors to family and close friends.
- In the second section, we'll consider how to mentor people outside the family yet close at hand: in your church or neighborhood or workplace—those you see on a regular basis.
- In the third section, we'll discuss how to mentor people who are on the margins of, or even outside of, our faith and cultures.

By the end of this chapter, you'll be equipped to be a mentor in your family, church, and world. Mentoring was, we know, Jesus' chosen way of reaching his faith-community and his world, by spending most of his time with a few people. This can be our way of reaching out, too, in our families, our faith-communities, and our world. We don't need to be a pastor or seminary trained in order to mentor. We can become mentors one-on-one with ever more faithful protégés—and, in turn, we'll become more faithful ourselves.

MENTORING FAMILY AND FRIENDS

Within our family, we are mentors, whether good or bad, examples of faith or the lack of it, teachers of generosity or greed. Parents and grandparents know this. Aunts and uncles know this. Mentoring within the family circle is at the fulcrum of faith. For indigenous peoples in the United States and around the world, for example, mentoring extends throughout the tribe through the role of the elders. As the Reverend Anita Phillips of the Keetoowah Cherokee nation explains, "Elders with many years of wisdom bring insight and leadership across time. They teach the younger generations to find the Creator and the holy in our sacred sites. They teach ceremonies and rituals that honor the earth."

Lucy Rider Meyer, whom we met in the last chapter, was mentored by a family member. Her commitment to Bible study was something she learned from her father. Meyer would recall the delight she felt when she heard him read Bible stories within her family circle.

> Born and trained in a [C]hristian home in the pure and quiet country, I was converted when thirteen years old. But I learned to love the Bible long before that time. It was a custom of my father's, to gather his whole large family about him of a winter evening, or a Sunday afternoon, and ask us questions concerning various Bible characters or events. I used to sit, one of that circle, in the great farm-house kitchen, in Vermont, watching for my turn, and answering or missing, as the case might be, the questions concerning Moses and David

and Paul. . . . [Also] my father used to tell us the Bible stories. No stories will ever thrill me again like the stories heard from my father's lips, in that same old wide-roomed farm house.[2]

Long before she founded Chicago Training School, this experience bore fruit, as Meyer brought her love for study of the Bible to her preparation for a Sunday school class of young boys. Her biographer notes: "Study was never a task. She loved it. She began a new book with the zest of a hungry man sitting down to a feast."[3] Meyer prepared Bible readings and lessons for her class. In one year alone, she wrote four thousand questions that arose while she prepared her Sunday school lessons. That's eleven questions a day, every day of the year—arising from Bible study! And who fired this love of scripture? A mentor. Someone from a prior generation. A father.

LOVING GOD WITH OUR MEMORIES

Mentoring within the family was the fulcrum of faith in the Israelite world. The center of the Old Testament is the *Shema*, a Hebrew word that means, "Hear," a call to faithfulness. Deuteronomy 6:4-9 reads like this:

> Hear, O Israel: The LORD is our God, the LORD alone. You shall love the LORD your God with all your heart, and with all your soul, and with all your might. Keep these words that I am commanding you today in your heart. Recite them to your children and talk about them when you are at home and when you are away, when you lie down and when you rise. Bind them as a sign on your hand, fix them as an emblem on your forehead, and write them on the doorposts of your house and on your gates.

When asked what the greatest command of scripture was, Jesus quoted the *Shema* without a moment's hesitation, "Hear, O Israel: the Lord our God, the Lord is one; you shall love the Lord your God with all your heart, and with all your soul, and with all your mind, and with all your strength" (Mark 12:29-30). Jesus quickly added another command from Leviticus 19:18, "You shall love your neighbor as yourself."

Ask yourself what loving God with your whole heart means, and you may come up with something like, "Love God with your whole self" or "your whole being" or "your whole commitment." That sounds good, but it doesn't quite get to the *heart* of the *Shema* in Deuteronomy 6. We think of the heart as the seat of emotions—or perhaps the will. Actually, this Hebrew word *lebab* (heart) would be better translated by the word *memory* as in "You shall love the LORD your God with all your *memory*." Two chapters earlier, in fact, this same Hebrew word is the word for memory. Deuteronomy 4:9 reads like this: "But take care and watch yourselves closely, so as neither to forget the things that your eyes have seen nor to let them slip from your mind [*lebab*] all the days of your life." This is a commandment to remember, never to forget, not to let something you've seen slip from your mind. The best sense of the word that is translated "mind," then, is memory: "But take care and watch yourselves closely, so as neither to forget the things that your eyes have seen nor to let them slip from your memory, your *lebab* . . .""

That's exactly what we are asked to do in Deuteronomy 6, the *Shema*. We love the Lord our God with our memories: "You shall love the LORD your God with all your heart . . . and "keep these words that I am commanding you today in your heart"—*in your memory*.

We say something like this often: "You need to learn these by heart." When I (Jack) tell my students at the beginning of my Introduction to Bible class the dates they need to learn—1280, 921, 721, 586 BCE and so forth—I warn them, "You'd better know these by heart!"

How does this happen? It's simple, according to what follows in the *Shema*: "make them known to your children and your children's children." We remember God's works by telling children about them. We remember by mentoring.

FROM MOTHER TO CHILD

As essential as this is for keeping and passing on the faith, it's not rocket science. The *Shema* continues, "talk about them when you are at home and when you are away, when you lie down and when you rise." This is what Lucy Rider Meyer's father did. And this is what Susanna Wesley, John and Charles's mother, did centuries ago. She set up a systematized religious training for her children, whose "spiritual nurture she looked upon as a sacred trust."[4] As soon as they turned five years old, Susanna began homeschooling her children, teaching them their letters along with religious training for six hours a day.

In a letter to John Wesley in 1732, she confided:

> Our children were taught, as soon as they could speak, the Lord's prayer, which they were made to say at rising and bedtime constantly; to which, as they grew bigger, were added a short prayer for their parents, and some collects, and some portion of Scripture, as their memories could bear. They were very early made to distinguish the Sabbath from other days, before they could well speak or go. They were as soon taught to be still at family prayers, and to ask a blessing immediately after, which they used to do by signs, before they could kneel or speak.[5]

As they grew older, she set aside a routine time to spend with each child. Susanna's regularity is staggering: "On Monday, I talk with Molly; on Tuesday, with Hetty; Wednesday, with Nancy; Thursday, with Jacky; Friday, with Patty; Saturday, with Charles; and with Emily and Sukey together, on Sunday."[6] She continued even when they were away from home. For Sukey, she wrote a long exposition on the Apostles' Creed, which she also sent to her son Samuel. She considered this a pressing duty of motherhood.

> When I have leisure, I think I cannot be better employed than in writing something that may be useful to my children; and though I know there are abundance of good books wherein these subjects are more fully and accurately treated of than I can pretend to write, yet I am willing to think that my children will somewhat regard what I can do for them, though the performance be mean; since they know it comes from their mother, who is perhaps more concerned for their eternal happiness than any one in the world.[7]

No, it's not rocket science, though for many of us latter-day Methodists, sports and music and schoolwork preempt the eternal work of soul-tending that nurtures us—and our children—if we love God with our memories. We don't need new skills to accomplish this, just new priorities.

PRACTICAL REMEMBRANCE

In fact, famed nineteenth-century Methodist evangelist Phoebe Palmer recalled her dinner time practice of requiring each person at the table to quote a Bible verse from memory following the letters of the alphabet. Her practice is like, "I'm going on a vacation and taking with me . . ." in which each person adds a new item with the next letter of the alphabet. At Phoebe Palmer's table, the first person chose a verse beginning with the letter "a," the next with the letter "b," and so on.[8] (Thankfully, the hungry crew didn't repeat each verse; the person whose verse began with "y" did not need to repeat all of the preceding verses. Dinner certainly would have gotten cold!)

The *Shema* recommends still another method to jog our memories: "Bind them [God's commands] as a sign on your hand, fix them as an emblem on your forehead, and write them on the doorposts of your house." This, too, is simple enough. Children love to paint by hand. Why not paint by hand while loving God by heart? Crafts can be geared to biblical stories, as often happens in Sunday school or vacation Bible school. It's done at summer camp all the time. Why not at home? Our homes can be filled with creative, artistic tokens of God that visually redirect our priorities and emblematize our commitments.

We can recite scripture, wear scripture, paint scripture onto our entryways. (The *mezuzah* on the doorpost of a Jewish family follows this command explicitly. Know what's inside? A small scroll with the *Shema* written on it!) The core of love for God is *not* emotional, *not* star gazing, *not* feeling. The core of love for God is committing to memory what God has done for us in every last detail of our blessed lives. This is the story we tell. This is the God whose words we recite, wear, and post as reminders of our faith.

A FAMILY ALTAR

We've been convinced as we've written this study to create something we wish we'd done years ago, when our children were young: make a family altar as a center for family devotions. In many nineteenth-century Methodist homes, families gathered around a home altar. Phoebe Palmer's family, for example, met at their home altar whenever the bell sounded to read the Bible, sing a hymn, and pray. Like many other altars, theirs contained a Bible, a hymn book, and a candle to read by. Not surprisingly, when she became America's leading preacher, the altar became a central metaphor in her call to a deeper experience of God. This experience began by laying one's all on the altar, so to speak, by consecrating oneself entirely to God, following the admonition of Romans 12:1: "Present your bodies as a living sacrifice, holy and acceptable to God." She believed that God accepted and sanctified whatever one placed upon the altar. "It is by Thy power alone, O God, that I am kept. Here shall I ever feel the cleansing efficacy. Here shall my soul fill and expand—fill and expand—till it shall burst its tenement, and faith shall be lost in sight."[9]

Another prominent Methodist, Frances Willard, who for nearly twenty years presided over the Woman's Christian Temperance Union, the largest woman's organization in the United States in the late nineteenth and early twentieth centuries, recalled family worship around a family altar that boasted religious pictures and mottoes, a Bible stand, even a miniature organ. The Willard family gathered regularly for morning prayers as well as informal Sunday evenings of hymn singing.

Katie Geneva Cannon, a leading voice among African-American theologians, recollects the power of family gatherings in her childhood home in North Carolina, especially during violent thunderstorms. "The Cannon household became—and still becomes—a folklore sanctuary," as her mother wove together slave stories, spirituals, and prayer.

> When the rainfall's intensity and the wind's velocity drop and the lightning and the thunder recede, I know that the end of the storytelling is near. Believing that a direct personal relationship with God exists, my mother always concludes her stories with a long prayer of intercession, praise, and thanksgiving. Kneeling beside the couch, she prays for the needs of both the immediate and the extended family. She celebrates God's goodness, majesty, and mercy. She frequently enunciates thanks for the gifts of the

earth and for all the blessings received. After a period of silence, my mother then provides times for every family member to bear witness to the immediate power of Jesus as "heart fixer and mind regulator."[10]

If these vignettes do not describe your family, then you can begin now. Take small steps to love God with your memories. Recite God's good works morning, noon, and night. (Remember here the regularity of prayer that we posed in Chapter 1.) Play memory games that are like Phoebe Palmer's dinnertime ritual. Paint and braid and build tokens to remember God's activity, and set them around your house. Build a family altar.

In Chapter 1, we urged you to create a welcoming, hospitable space for prayer and learning. The principle is the same for a family altar: create a warm and welcoming space, with items from each family member, to which the whole family can be drawn.

So this summer, years later than we should have, we are creating a family altar in our kitchen. We have a small homemade table built by Jack and the kids from 4x4s and scraps of old plywood; it's painted red, a kid's color. We have a plant on it, a bowl of fruit, and the normal bits and pieces of family life, like magazines tossed away and half-read newspapers. Off they go, consigned to another corner of the kitchen or the recycle bin. In their place, we'll put candles, a Bible (probably *The Message* because of its value for oral reading), a hymn book, one favorite book from each of us that focuses our faith, and perhaps some other tokens of faith. We're by no means a perfect family, loving God with our memories. And that—yes, precisely that—is why we need a family altar.

MENTORING THE TYPICAL PEOPLE IN OUR LIVES

THE MIRACLE OF MULTIPLICATION

During my first month as a freshman in college, I (Jack) went to the floor lounge of the dorm, where a sophomore was talking about a Bible study he would lead. I was mesmerized and joined up. I got much more than I bargained for. Kenny began to mentor me. We memorized scripture together, prayed together, and ate in the cafeteria together each week. More than that, Kenny believed in what he called the "with principle," so he invited me along to activities he thought would benefit me. During spring term, for instance, we walked every Sunday night to nearby DuPage County Jail, where we talked with inmates, many of whom were awaiting trial for severe crimes.

What Kenny did required no special expertise, no seminary training, no advanced degree. What Kenny did required a willingness to read the Bible together, to be open in prayer together—and the forethought to invite someone to events he was already attending. *You can do this.* Each and every one of us can do this. In fact, the genius of United Methodist Women is that you are already organized to promote exactly this sort of mentoring.

Kenny, in fact, would often talk about the "multiplication principle." "If you mentor [he called it discipling] someone for six months," he'd tell me, "and both of you mentor someone for six months and all four of you mentor someone for six months, by the end of ten years, you will have helped over a million Christians to be equipped to follow Jesus better." Yes, you read that right: over a million Christians active in prayer, Bible study, and social transformation. It's simple math. It's explosive math. It's math that all of us can do. Here, in fact, is Kenny's chart, just in case you can't fathom the miracle of multiplication:

Year 1	1 (mentor) +1 (protégé)=2	2 (mentors) +2 (protégés) =4
Year 2	4 (mentors) +4 (protégés) =8	8+8=16
Year 3	16+16=32	32+32=64
Year 4	64+64=128	128+128=256
Year 5	512 (total involved)	1,024
Year 6	2,048	4,096
Year 7	8,192	16,384
Year 8	32,768	65,536
Year 9	131,072	262, 144
Year 10	524,288	1,048,576

Here's how it works. In year one, you mentor one person for six months, then both of you mentor one person for six months. By the end of year one, four people are equipped as mentors. In year two, all four of you mentor others for six months—for a total of eight people involved—then all eight mentor others for six months, giving a total of sixteen people prepared to mentor, to "make disciples." And so forth, so that by the end of the tenth year, over a million Christians will be equipped to mentor other Christians.

All this takes is for us to realize we can be mentors, and the perfect place to start is right smack in the middle of United Methodist Women. *Set your priorities so that you will pray with, study with, be with, and change the world with one other person for six months.* All it takes is spending an hour or two with one person a week, praying, studying, and then doing what you'd normally do—but *with* that other person.

If you're at all worried about how you would pray and what you would study, we've already given you suggestions in the first two chapters. Start simply, perhaps with listening prayer. For study, practice *lectio divina* together. Whatever you do, go ahead, put those chapters into practice, not just by yourself, but with someone younger or newer to the faith than yourself.

MENTORS ON A MISSION

Scripture is rich with models of mentoring. In the early church, for example, an exceptional model of mentoring is Barnabas, whose nickname, by the way, was "Son of Encouragement" (Acts 4:36-37). Barnabas became a mentor to the apostle Paul. This took some courage because of Paul's reputation for persecuting Christians. When Paul attempted to cozy up to Jesus' followers in Jerusalem, "they were all afraid of him" and mistrusted him. "But Barnabas took him, brought him to the apostles, and described for them how on the road he had seen the Lord." As a result, Paul "went in and out among them in Jerusalem" (Acts 9:26-28). Barnabas, in short, took the risk of association.

Later, Barnabas was sent up to Antioch because the church was growing like a weed. Even though he himself was "full of the Holy Spirit and of faith," quite capable of teaching the new believers in Antioch, "Barnabas went to Tarsus to look for Saul, and when he had found him, he brought him to Antioch. So it was that for an entire year they met with the church and taught a great many people" (Acts 11:24-26). Barnabas had already brought Paul into communion with the church in Jerusalem. Now he goes in search of Paul so that *they* can teach together. How better to learn—and to get to know someone well—than to teach together? There is a certain grace in shared labor.

Apparently Paul and Barnabas remained close associates, tandem workers in the harvest, because later on, while the church in Antioch was "worshiping the Lord and fasting, the Holy Spirit said, 'Set apart for me Barnabas and Saul for the work to which I have called them'" (Acts 13:2). Off they went *together* on their (not just *Paul's*) first missionary journey.

Later still, when the influx of Gentiles—believers who didn't observe Jewish Torah, eat kosher, or circumcise baby boys—was nearly overwhelming, some strict Jewish believers demanded that male Gentile converts be circumcised. Whom do we find fighting with them to let people in the church without this restriction? Paul and Barnabas, of course. "And after Paul and Barnabas had no small dissension and debate with them," Luke writes, "Paul and Barnabas and some of the others were appointed to go up to Jerusalem to discuss this question with the apostles and the elders" (Acts 15:2). Compromise was reached, universal circumcision avoided, and the head of the Jerusalem church wrote a letter, sent by Judas and Silas, but accompanied, too, by "our beloved Barnabas and Paul, who have risked their lives for the sake of our Lord Jesus Christ" (Acts 15:25-26).

In North America, at least, we are a community of individuals. In scripture, by way of contrast, tasks are often accomplished in pairs—sometimes equal pairs, sometimes a mentor with a protégé, sometimes, as we'll soon see, a married couple. Incorporating this insight into our lives may require a shift from seeing ourselves as individuals or group members or church members to seeing ourselves yoked together with another person for the good of the gospel.

Such pairing doesn't always promise smooth sailing. After the compromise over circumcision was reached, after Paul and Barnabas were sent to Antioch along with Judas and Silas, Paul and Barnabas had a vicious falling out. Barnabas wanted to take John Mark, but Paul didn't because John Mark had deserted them earlier. "The disagreement became so sharp that they parted company," Luke tells us. "Barnabas took Mark with him. . . . But Paul chose Silas and set out" (Acts 15:39-40). Notice this: even when they split sharply, believers headed out in pairs, Paul with Silas, Barnabas with Mark. Such is the centripetal force of leading-through-mentoring at the headwaters of Christianity.

Yes, there will be bumps in the road. No, not every relationship you develop will be long-lasting. Still, mentoring is a wonderful *and biblical* way to strengthen your faith as you foster another's. Barnabas did what he would have done anyway: taught, talked about his experiences, and traveled. He just chose to do these things *with* Paul and, when that didn't work, *with* Mark. Small wonder the early believers nicknamed him Son of Encouragement.

MENTORING UNEXPECTED PEOPLE

A Methodist minister's wife in Milledgeville, Georgia, Etta Pursely Barton, made it a habit to invite to church students from other countries enrolled at the Georgia State College for Women. Through this practice, she became lifelong friends with two Korean women, Chungil Choo and Chinsook Kwon, both of whom were followers of Confucius when they met Barton. Choo and Kwon were among the first students to come to the United States after the liberation of Korea from Japanese imperial rule in 1945.[11] Nine months after they first met Etta Barton and before they returned to Korea toward the end of the war, Choo and Kwon converted to Christianity. At their baptisms in the Milledgeville First Methodist Church, they wore their traditional Korean attire.

In a letter to Barton, Choo wrote about how much her new faith meant to her when she attended church the morning after hearing that war had begun in her country. "We were almost overcome with grief and knew not what to do. But, kneeling at the altar of the church in prayer, we received strength and comfort. We then were able to get up and go on with our studies with the hope and faith that a better day would dawn for our people." She also commented in retrospect that the Bartons never forced their faith on her. What impressed her was their hospitality, how they opened up their home to foreign students every Christmas and treated them like family. "Never before in our lives," wrote Choo, "had we been offered by anybody who was not related closely to us by blood, color, race, or otherwise the kind of generosity that the Bartons showed us that day."[12]

These relationships, in turn, had a profound impact on Barton. Through Kwon's and Choo's letters to her written from Korea during the war's final months, she came to understand the conflict from a more personal perspective than most Americans. She wrote to Kwon and Choo that she and her friends "are seeing the liberation of Seoul as a more personal matter since they know you and are interested in the welfare of your people. You have made a wonderful contribution to world brotherhood as you have walked the ways of America." Because of her friendship with Choo and Kwon, Barton began a foundation to provide financial aid for students from overseas to study in the United States. She also mounted a campaign in the South to fight racism against Asians. A decade after first meeting Choo and Kwon, Barton wrote, "They have broadened our horizon and deepened our faith so we give thanks to God for sending Korea to us."[13]

The relationship between Ella Barton, Chungil Choo, and Chinsook Kwon illustrates that the privilege of mentoring demands a keen eye, an alert mind, a heart for hospitality. Not every possible protégé will belong to your family or church community. There are also, as the early church discovered, unexpected people to mentor.

THE RIGHT KIND OF PROTÉGÉ

After the first persecution in the history of the church, one of the leaders in the earliest Jerusalem church, Philip, headed to Samaria, where he had an extremely successful mission. Lots of Samaritans believed in Jesus, among them Simon the magician, whom the Samaritans nicknamed "Great" and "the Power of God" (Acts 8:9-10). Even though Philip was surrounded by all sorts of people, experiences, and overwhelming success, *he closely associated with only one person in Samaria*: a former magician who, as we'll see, made a terrible mistake! Yet that one person teaches us a lot about what to look for in a protégé. These, according to the story of Philip and Simon, are the sort of people to mentor.

Someone willing to be devoted to a mentor. Simon "was devoted to" Philip (see Acts 8:12-13, our translation). This verb, *be devoted to*, signaled the depth of Simon's commitment to Philip. Jesus' followers *devoted themselves* to prayer (1:14); after Pentecost, they *devoted themselves* to the apostles' teaching and other signs of unity (2:42); daily they *devoted themselves* to one another in the temple (2:46); the apostles *devoted themselves* to prayer and serving the word (6:4). This is deep, regular devotion. Now, in Samaria, Simon exercised no less devotion to Philip. (English translations, such as NRSV, unfortunately translate the same Greek word with different English words in the passages we refer to here. The Greek uses the same verb in Acts 1:14, 2:42, 2:46, 6:4, and 8:12-13, so we have translated the same Greek word with the same English words, "be devoted to," in every instance. In this way, you can see the powerful sense of devotion that connected Simon to Philip.)

Someone willing to learn. Like other Samaritans, Simon "listened eagerly" to Philip (8:6), even though, prior to Philip's arrival, the Samaritans had "listened eagerly" to Simon (8:11). Simon displayed no hints of jealousy; instead, he stuck to Philip like glue (8:13).

Someone willing to change. The apostles heard about Philip's success in Samaria, so they traveled from Jerusalem to impart the Holy Spirit to the Samaritans. Simon the magician, not knowing better, "offered them money, saying, 'Give me also this power so that anyone on whom I lay my hands may receive the Holy Spirit'" (8:18-19). Simon was absolutely wrong-headed. Buy the Holy Spirit? Really?

Peter responded viciously, consigning Simon, and his money with him, to hell. Simon reacted with genuine repentance. "Pray for me to the Lord," he begged, "that nothing of what you have said may happen to me" (8:24). Simon turned on a dime.

Simon's responses to Philip and Peter show us what to look for in someone to mentor. Don't necessarily look for protégés who have it all right—the perfect believers, the careful ones, the good church people. Instead:

- Keep your eyes peeled for those willing to be devoted.
- Identify people who are willing to learn.
- Work with people who are willing to change.

A knack for discovering unlikely protégés has characterized great mentors throughout history. Look again, for example, at Lucy Rider Meyer, who spearheaded the Methodist deaconess movement. Most of the women who enrolled in the Chicago Training School, which she founded, came from rural farms in Iowa, river towns in Ohio, and one-street villages in Illinois. Some had been schoolteachers; others were fairly illiterate. These unlikely women had not encountered a metropolis except in their imagination. Yet, to the great urban centers—Chicago, New York City, San Francisco—they came, looking for an opportunity to put their faith into action. In these cities, with unsanitary and overcrowded tenements housing new arrivals from southern and eastern Europe, they would learn to nurse a torn and tattered humanity, school an unlearned child, equip an expectant mother, interpret for the immigrant, and tell everyone about Jesus.

One of the women who enrolled in the deaconess training school came from a small town, where her family and friends had become accustomed to her severe speech impediment. Meyer, ever the capable mentor, recognized that this speech impediment would be a serious obstacle to the young woman's work as a deaconess. Rather than sending the woman back home—the path of least resistance—Meyer opted to give her a chance. Within several weeks, others noticed that the woman's speech had improved by leaps and bounds. How? "Mrs. Meyer herself had been giving her private lessons in proper enunciation. The young woman's assignment in housework was to sweep the dormitory in which Mrs. Meyer's room was located. At half-past six every morning Mrs. Meyer took her into her room and gave her a half hour of carefully directed exercises in articulation."[14]

Perfect protégés don't exist. Willing ones do. Find them.

THE RIGHT KIND OF MENTOR

If we return to the story of Philip, we see that he allowed Simon's faith to develop at its own pace, even if that faith was immature. Luke signaled this immaturity by writing, "After being baptized, he [*was devoted to*] Philip and was amazed when he saw the signs and great miracles that took place" (Acts 8:13). It's just possible that Simon was dazzled by miracles; Philip, it seems, didn't mind. Peter, in contrast, did. He bristled with impatience when Simon offered to buy the rights to the Holy Spirit. Philip, as far as we can tell, remained silent.

We see Philip's huge capacity to mentor unexpected people even more vividly in the next episode, when he encountered an Ethiopian eunuch on a wilderness road. In this unlikely scene, Philip was a terrific model of how to be an effective mentor. Let's follow the story to see how we can be effective mentors, too.

- "Then an angel of the Lord said to Philip, 'Get up and go toward the south to the road that goes down from Jerusalem to Gaza.' (This is a wilderness road.) So he got up and went" (Acts 8:26-27). We may not hear an angel, but we can be open to finding ourselves in surprising places. Be adventurous. To find unexpected people, you'll need to look in unexpected places.
- "Then the Spirit said to Philip, 'Go over to this chariot and join it'" (Acts 8:29). This simple statement says a boatload about the impulse for mentoring. We don't know how the Spirit spoke to Philip, but we do know that Philip listened. We've given you a handful of strategies in the first and second chapters for putting yourself in a position—in a *condition*, really—to listen for the Holy Spirit.
- "So Philip ran up to it" (Acts 8:30). You have to love Philip. After all he'd been through, he was still eager for the next step in his adventure with God. He didn't drag his heels. He didn't walk. He *ran*. Being a great mentor demands (and creates) enthusiasm.
- Philip "heard him [the eunuch] reading the prophet Isaiah. He asked, 'Do you understand what you are reading?'" (Acts 8:30). Philip takes the initiative in the conversation. A mentor needs to be ready to take the initiative to develop a relationship. Nothing fancy. A simple question will do.
- The eunuch replied, "'How can I, unless someone guides me?' And he invited Philip to get in and sit beside him" (Acts 8:31). Philip listened to the eunuch's question and responded to his request. Mentoring is not all one way. A good mentor is responsive to a protégé's questions and requests.

- "The eunuch asked Philip, 'About whom, may I ask you, does the prophet say this, about himself or about someone else?' Then Philip began to speak, and starting with this scripture, he proclaimed to him the good news about Jesus" (Acts 8:34-35). Another question! And together they sat, studied the scriptures, and talked.

Picture this pair sitting side by side, a black man and a (relatively) white man, a sexually crippled man (a eunuch) and a robust man with four daughters (Acts 21:9), bouncing along in a chariot on a desolate road, united solely by the scroll of Isaiah that is draped over their knees. It's a sight to behold.

Now *that* is an image of mentoring you can carry with you. An unexpected pair, a shared scroll, an out-of-the-way location, yet at the very center of God's work. One by unexpected one, the people of God grew. One by surprising one, the church of God was enriched. And why? Because Philip found himself in unexpected places, listened to the Spirit, was eager to mentor, was willing to take the initiative, was open to questions and requests, and was contented to sit and study scripture at another person's pace. Yes, *that* is the portrait of a mentor you can take with you.

QUITE A PAIR, QUITE A PROTÉGÉ

Priscilla and Aquila stand out in scripture as model mentors, people, as Paul puts it, "who risked their necks for my life" (Romans 16:4). Refugees in Corinth who'd been thrown out of Rome because of an imperial persecution of Jews—away from home themselves—they still managed to host Paul for a couple of years in their home away from home. Their hospitality, in fact, extended to entire churches; Paul sends greetings to the Corinthians from Priscilla and Aquila, "together with the church in their house" (1 Corinthians 16:19).

It's not surprising, given their bent for hospitality, that, when they overheard the powerful but not-quite-right teaching of a Jew named Apollos, Priscilla and Aquila took him home. Here's how the story goes:

Now there came to Ephesus a Jew named Apollos, a native of Alexandria. He was an eloquent man, well-versed in the scriptures.

He had been instructed in the Way of the Lord; and he spoke with burning enthusiasm and taught accurately the things concerning Jesus, though he knew only the baptism of John. He began to speak boldly in the synagogue; but when Priscilla and Aquila heard him, they took him aside and explained the Way of God to him more accurately. And when he wished to cross over to Achaia, the believers encouraged him and wrote to the disciples to welcome him. (Acts 18:24-27)

Three verbs, three key verbs, tell us how Aquila and Priscilla mentored Apollos—and how we can mentor others, even unexpected others, today.

- They *listened* to him.
- They *took* him.
- They *taught* him more accurately.

As we saw in the story of Philip and the Ethiopian eunuch, *listening* is often the first step in mentoring. Good teachers know their students' questions, concerns, and commitments, because they listen first.

They then took the initiative. Philip ran to the chariot; Aquila and Priscilla took Apollos aside. The translation, "took aside," is too bland a description of what this remarkable couple did. They actually "took him home." They didn't sidle up to Apollos during coffee hour or after morning worship, pull him aside, and correct him on the spot. Not at all. They showed him warm hospitality. This verb, *take,* is used of eating, of taking nourishment into bodies (Acts 27:33, 36). It's translated by the word *welcome*, to depict warm hospitality after a shipwreck: "The natives [of Malta] showed us unusual kindness. Since it had begun to rain and was cold, they kindled a fire and *welcomed* all of us around it" (Acts 28:2, emphasis added). They welcomed cold and wet and quite unwelcome guests by taking them in and perching them around a warm fire. Now that's hospitality. And that's just what Aquila and Priscilla offered Apollos. Think a home-cooked meal, a comfy couch, and a convivial conversation.

In the warmth and welcome of their home, Priscilla and Aquila taught (this is the third verb) Apollos more accurately what he knew only partially.

In fact, Luke puts it perfectly: Apollos taught the people "accurately"; Priscilla and Aquila taught him "more accurately." There is affirmation here, an acknowledgment of what is right, in order to pave the way for correction. There is gentleness here, hospitality, and only then teaching further truth.

We've seen this scenario before in Philip, who allowed Simon the Magician to stick to him like glue yet grow at his own pace. We've seen something else: a protégé with a willingness to learn, to change. Simon stood corrected in the face of Peter. Now Priscilla and Aquila begin with what is accurate in what Apollos was teaching and teach him from that point. And Apollos accepts more accurate teaching without an ounce of defensiveness. The result is stunning: the whole group of believers encouraged Apollos and wrote a letter to believers at his next destination to commend him enthusiastically.

Even ministers can benefit from mentoring! In the early, settling-in years of Methodism in America, women provided hospitality to circuit-riding, itinerant preachers. Along with providing food and shelter, as Methodist historian, Russell Richey, explains, these women "were supporters, confidants, spiritual directors, counselors, confessors, 'mothers,' tutors. . . ." Take Sarah Ennalls, for instance, who mentored an itinerant preacher, Henry Boehm. By his own account, she prevented him from quitting the ministry.

> Mrs. Ennalls, who was a person of discernment, saw I was suffering under deep depression of spirits. I was fearful I had mistaken my calling. Ingenuously she asked me a great many questions, till she drew from me the real state of my mind. . . . Then she exhorted me in the most earnest and emphatic manner not to abandon my work, but to keep on. I resolved in the strength of my Master to try again, and though over threescore years have gone into eternity since "having obtained help from God, I continue unto this day." Well I remember that hospitable mansion; and the room in which we were, the attitude of the woman, her anxious countenance, her piercing eye, the tone of her voice, are all before me just as if it were yesterday. Her wise counsel has had an influence upon me all my days; it shaped my destiny for life.[15]

Once again, we've come across great mentors, who listen, host, and teach through affirmation. We've met a receptive—if not quite correct—protégé with a learner's heart. And we've seen the remarkable result of this relationship: a teacher in the church who, Luke goes on to say, "greatly helped those who through grace had become believers" (Acts 18:27).

Before turning to the next page, before diving into the next chapter, take a few deep breaths. When you've settled in, when the monkeys in the tree have stopped chattering, consider what kind of mentor you can be, whom you can mentor, whether you are even open to becoming a mentor. If, as you listen, you are open to, even excited by, the possibility of becoming a mentor in the faith—and we've laid out for you plenty of examples—then set your gaze, widening it at each turn, on your family, on United Methodist Women, on an unlikely group of people. What better way to become, as the PURPOSE of United Methodist Women says, "a community of women whose purpose is to know God and to experience freedom as whole persons through Jesus Christ; to develop a creative, supportive fellowship; and to expand concepts of mission through participation in the global ministries of the church."

CHAPTER 4

Transform

Many are we now, and one, we who Jesus have put on;
there is neither bond nor free, male nor female, Lord, in thee.

Love, like death, hath all destroyed, rendered all distinctions void;
names and sects and parties fall; thou, O Christ, art all in all! [1]
–Charles Wesley

Ida B. Wells-Barnett seated herself in the women's car of the train. This was her custom, but the conductor refused her ticket and ordered her into the smoking car with other African Americans. When she refused to move, at the next stop three men threw her off the train, to a standing ovation and applause from the white passengers. The first court decision awarded her $500 in damages. In retaliation, the railroad company appealed the decision—and won.

In a diary entry dated April 11, 1887, she described her reaction to the Tennessee Supreme Court's decision to overturn her lawsuit against the Chesapeake and Ohio Railroad.

The Supreme Court reversed the decision of the lower court in my behalf . . . I had hoped such great things from my suit for my people generally. I have firmly believed all along that the law was on our side and would, when we appealed to it, give us justice. I feel shorn of that belief and utterly discouraged, and just now if it were possible would gather my race in my arms and fly far away with them. O God is there no redress, no peace, no justice in this land for us? Thou hast always fought the battles of the weak and oppressed. Come to my aid at this moment and teach me what to do, for I am sorely, bitterly disappointed. Show us the way, even as Thou led the children of Israel out of bondage into the promised land.[2]

Wells-Barnett, born a slave and emancipated with her family when she was three years old, was raised in the southern black Methodist church. Early on, she developed a deep spirituality, a strong belief in God's nearness in Jesus Christ. She also possessed a strong sense of Christian duty made visible in high moral standards and in the doing of good works. In a diary entry, she found herself wanting when she measured herself by these standards and prayed to God for greater faithfulness. "While there I reviewed my last year of existence and I am so overwhelmed with the little I have done for one who has done so much for me. . . . I shall begin this year with that determination, so that another year may find me with more to offer the master in the way of good works."[3]

These commitments coalesced in the courage, persistence, and creative maladjustment she later applied to her advocacy of the anti-lynching movement and racial justice. From 1892, when her close friend, Thomas Moss, was lynched in Memphis, Wells-Barnett became a national and international critic of lynching, both in speech and in her work as a journalist. Because she viewed the anti-lynching movement as a moral issue, she expected that "all Christian and moral forces" would do all they could to exercise high moral standards of justice, which she held personally, to support it. For instance, she urged business owners not to invest their capital in places where mob violence ruled, and she denounced southerners for equating the lynching of a black man with "slaying a mad dog." Nor did she let northerners off the hook. She condemned their silence as complicity: "Is not the North by its seeming acquiescence as responsible morally as the South is criminally for the awful lynching record of the past thirteen years?"[4] She even criticized African Americans for sitting back and not voicing or acting out their protest.

Wells-Barnett never lost faith that God was on the side of the oppressed and that people would act according to high moral standards. When she visited twelve African American men who were sentenced to be electrocuted for their alleged role in a riot while attempting to organize a labor union—a decision handed down in six minutes—she urged them to turn to "the God of Paul and Silas who opened their prison gates, and if you have all the faith you say you have, you ought to believe that he will open your prison doors too." Further, she encouraged the men to pray for the "judges who have to pass on your cases [that they] will be given the wisdom and courage to decide in your behalf."[5]

Her unrelenting commitment to racial justice met with heavy resistance. After she published a newspaper article exposing inequalities in the black schools in Memphis, she lost her teaching job. The conflict grew more violent after she wrote an editorial about interracial relationships. While she was out of town, the office of the *Free Speech*, a newspaper of which she was part owner, was vandalized and demolished, and lynching threats were published against her in another newspaper.

Resistance arose from unexpected quarters as well. Wells-Barnett butted heads with Frances Willard, president of the Woman's Christian Temperance Union (WCTU). Wells-Barnett claimed that "only after Negroes are in prison for crimes that efforts of these temperance women are exerted without regard to 'race, color, or previous condition.'" Willard, in turn, fed the conflict by describing southern African Americans as a "great dark faced mob."[6] Some WCTU delegates tried to pass an anti-lynching declaration, but the WCTU, under the influence of Willard, refused to approve a public statement condemning lynching.

There are countless strategies that lead to the transformation of church and world. Reformers throughout the ages have taken all sorts of approaches to renewal. We will, in this chapter, outline one model, which can be discerned in scripture and in the lives of women such as Ida B. Wells-Barnett. This model contains three essential elements of transformation that can prompt people in all walks of life to transform their church and world: preparation, transformation, and readiness for resistance. Wells-Barnett experienced all three. Raised with deep spiritual commitments and high moral standards, she took concrete steps, as diverse as publishing newspaper articles, visiting prisoners, and working through massive women's organizations, to make those personal standards public. As a result, she met with resistance from various quarters, some predictable, others surprising.

These three elements—preparation, transformation, and resistance—are as basic as the gospel story itself. The first words Jesus heard are evidence of his preparation. After being baptized in the Jordan River, he heard the words of scripture echo in his ears: "You are my Son, the Beloved; with you I am well pleased." These words are straight from the pages of scripture—Isaiah 42:1 and Psalm 2:7, to be exact—just like Jesus' first sermon at Nazareth, where he quotes from Isaiah 61:1-3, with a smidgeon of Isaiah 58, about oppressed people, inserted smack in the middle. Armed with a conviction he had learned from scripture, Jesus spent his days caring for the oppressed, healing the sick, welcoming outcasts, and challenging those who had the ability to change the plight of the poor. As a result, he met with resistance and died a criminal's death.

AN ANONYMOUS PROPHET, AN INSPIRED SERVANT

This pattern characterized many of Israel's prophets. Amos had five modest visions (locusts, fire, a plumb line, fruit, and a crumbled altar) that led him to challenge Israel's Northern Kingdom with vivid language and turns of phrase, only to be ordered to go back home to the South. Ezekiel, a well-educated priest, had spectacular visions that led him to excoriate Israel for its desecration of the Temple, only to be ridiculed and ignored. Jeremiah, called in the most mundane of ways—seeing a pot tipped over and an almond branch—cajoled Israel with sermons and symbolic gestures, only to be rejected and even tossed down a well.

Any of these prophets model a pattern of preparation-transformation-resistance, but we'll focus our attention on an anonymous prophet, an inspired servant whose brilliant words are preserved in Isaiah 40–55. These stanzas of dazzling poetry in Isaiah 40–55 were probably composed during the Babylonian Exile, at some point between 587 and 539 BCE, when Israel was weary to the bone and mired in hopelessness. The Babylonian Empire had attacked, turned the Temple into shambles and exiled the king, along with other powerful Israelites, in utter humiliation.

Into the dark of this national tragedy, while Israel was in the throes of exile, an anonymous prophet tried to instill in his people the belief that they were on the cusp of liberation. No one could possibly have believed him.

Probably no one *even wanted* to believe him. Why? Because this prophet put his hope, not in an Israelite king on the throne of David, but in a foreign ruler, Cyrus, emperor of Persia. The prophet even calls the Persian Cyrus a "messiah" ("anointed") in Isaiah 45:1. In short, this prophet traced salvation in the future to an oppressor not a liberator, to a foreign empire rather than his own nation, to an alien emperor rather than Israel's messiah.

Yet this prophet was right. Salvation did not come from his own nation, his own people, his own king. Salvation came from another nation, another people, another ruler. In 539 BCE, Cyrus, ruler of Persia, issued a decree—a decree that is housed in the British Museum in cuneiform on a clay tablet—that exiled nations should return to their homelands.[7] Yes, the prophet was right. Back to Jerusalem Israel was allowed to return. Who would have believed it, and how did he know something that everyone else missed?

PREPARATION

The prophet knew because he committed himself to a daily regimen, which he describes for us:

> The Lord GOD has given me
>   the tongue of a learner,
> that I may know how to sustain
>   the weary with a word.
> Morning by morning [God] wakens—
>   wakens my ear
>   to listen as those who are taught.
> The Lord GOD has opened my ear,
>   and I was not rebellious,
>   I did not turn backward. (Isaiah 50:4-5)

The prophet, in this autobiographical snippet, offers a peek into how we prepare to become people of vision, agents of transformation.

First, God arouses the prophet morning by morning. Not once a week or twice a year on special holidays. Not just with other people around. Not only in a worship setting. Not when he feels like it. *Every* day.

The prophet prayed, not in a babble of words or a rampage of requests, but in the way we prompted in Chapter 1. He listened. He listened every day.

If you are earnest about taking part in the engine of transformation, at the beginning of every day—or whatever part of the day works best for you—simply listen. As we covered in Chapter 1, still your mind by breathing or by repeating a verse of scripture—or by incorporating any of the number of suggestions we offered. Then, in the quiet, like the prophet, listen for God to speak.

You can see that we've come full circle. A clear vision, a correct vision about God's activity in the world, doesn't always begin with doing. It doesn't always start with talking. It doesn't always take shape in preaching. The ability to embrace a clear vision, an alternative vision that flies in the face of everyone around us, begins with listening.

Second, the prophet listens with the ear of a disciple, of an eager learner, to receive God's teaching. This Hebrew word is worth looking hard at. The Hebrew noun *limmud*, which is translated "disciple," is related to the Hebrew verb *lamad* (see the shared letters *l* and *m* and *d* ?), which means "to teach and train." In the Book of Deuteronomy, parents are told to *teach* the Torah (Genesis through Deuteronomy) to their children, "talking about [it] when you are at home and when you are away, when you lie down and when you rise" (11:19; see 4:1, 5). God *teaches* the prophet scripture, just as parents are to teach their children scripture.

We've come full circle again. We'll see in a moment how the prophet's vision—and remember, his vision was *right*, as we can see from that artifact in the British Museum—was shaped by the scripture he studied. This realization takes us back to Chapter 2 and the importance of learning. Transformation isn't social justice separated from scripture. Scripture, rightly understood, propels us to all sorts of transformation. Our lives should be changed in light of scripture's vision of personal holiness. Our churches should be changed in light of scripture's vision of unity *and* diversity. Society should be changed in light of scripture's vision of God's penchant for justice. Even our environment should be changed, nurtured, in light of scripture's vision of the goodness of all creation.

We don't simply receive visions in spontaneous revelations, though these do indeed occur. We also receive a vision through the study of scripture if, like the prophet, daily *we listen* and *learn*.

TRANSFORMATION

There is a third part of the prophet's daily devotion that fires his vision: he listens in order to "know how to sustain the weary with a word." He listens in order to encourage—to in-courage or instill courage—a nation of weary exiles. How does he sustain the weary, encourage the done-in? By preparing them for the change ahead, for a homecoming they can't possibly yet imagine, for an event that's beyond their wildest dreams.

Simply put, the prophet speaks dazzling words of *transformation*. Think for a moment about that word *trans-form*: changing from one form to another. As in *trans*-portation: changing locations. Or *trans*-ition: changing states. This prophet understands that change is difficult, frightening, often unimaginable. Even positive change, good transition, beneficial transformation.

Where do these life-changing words come from? Scripture, of course. The prophet's vision is rife with Israel's ancient traditions, rooted in Israel's scripture—yet always in a new key, always shaped to shape the future, always extended to bring hope to the exiles. Notice his fresh take on the Exodus; we'll number the lines so that we can grasp the prophet's reinvention of scripture:

1. Awake, awake, put on strength,
2. O arm of the LORD!
3. Awake, as in days of old,
4. the generations of long ago!
5. Was it not you who cut Rahab in pieces,
6. who pierced the dragon?
7. Was it not you who dried up the sea,
8. the waters of the great deep;
9. who made the depths of the sea a way
10. for the redeemed to cross over?
11. So the ransomed of the LORD shall return,
12. and come to Zion with singing;
13. everlasting joy shall be upon their heads;
14. they shall obtain joy and gladness,
15. and sorrow and sighing shall flee away. (Isaiah 51:9-11)

The prophet begins, in lines 1-3, with a wake-up call. The exiles are asleep, unaware of God's movement, oblivious to God's power. They are, in short, in dire need of transformation.

He continues, in lines 4-8, where the world starts: long ago, when God wrestled the waters of creation into order. He begins with a view of creation you can't find in Genesis 1: creating land through the destruction of great monsters, like Rahab and the dragon. By dominating enemies, God tames the abyss of Genesis 1:1-2 and dries up the sea, creating land, just like on the third day of creation, when God separated water from land.

But wait. Creation turns to the Exodus in lines 7-10. The great abyss of Genesis 1 becomes the Egyptian Sea of Exodus 14–15. The drying of the abyss becomes the drying of the Red Sea. It's not Adam and Eve who walk on land but "the redeemed," the rescued slaves who scurry away from Egypt. The miracle of the Creation is also the miracle of the Exodus.

But wait again. Lines 11-15 wrap up Creation and Exodus into a vision of the future. Creation-Exodus becomes return from exile. "So the ransomed of the LORD shall return," the prophet sees, "and come to Zion with singing." God created the world. God liberated slaves. God would create and liberate again, returning exiles to their homes, with eternal joy crowning their heads—which is exactly what God did in 539 BCE through the unlikely hand of Cyrus the Persian.

You don't need to reinvent the wheel to transform your church, your world, the society you live in. It's there in listening. It's there in learning. It's there in scripture taken to a new key.

RESISTANCE

For all of the depth of his study, for the richness of his imagination, for the powerful word he offered the weary, for being absolutely right with his prediction, the prophet wasn't lifted on Israel's shoulders and taken ceremoniously back to Jerusalem. No. His message was met with untold, unrestrained resistance. Woven into the prophet's magnificent—and entirely correct—vision is pain and anguish. You can detect this under the surface of the first description of the prophet:

Here is my servant, whom I uphold,
  my chosen, in whom my soul delights;
I have put my spirit upon him;
  he will bring forth justice to the nations.
He will not cry or lift up his voice,
  or make it heard in the street;
a bruised reed he will not break,
  and a dimly burning wick he will not quench;
  he will faithfully bring forth justice.
He will not grow faint or be crushed
  until he has established justice in the earth;
  and the coastlands wait for his teaching [*torah*].
                                    (Isaiah 42:1-4)

Just look at the line, "He will not *grow faint* or be *crushed until*. . . ." Failure, weariness, exhaustion characterize the prophet. The words "cry out" refer to cries of anguish, as they do in the prediction that "you shall cry out for pain of heart, and shall wail for anguish of spirit" (Isaiah 65:14; see also 19:20; 33:7). The prophet won't give outward expression to anguish, won't cry out "in the street." This will be private pain, personal heartache. This prophet will persist, inspired yet nearly expired, "until he has established justice in the earth; / and the coastlands wait for his teaching" (Isaiah 42:4).

Resistance is also public and physical. He recalls: "I gave my back to those who struck me, / and my cheeks to those who pulled out the beard; / I did not hide my face / from insult and spitting" (Isaiah 50:5-6). Spitting, insults, and blows are the prophet's reward for a righteous vision.

In the end, he becomes a suffering servant, despised, rejected, a man of sorrows and acquainted with sickness, one from whom others hide, despised, of no account, struck down, afflicted, wounded, crushed, punished, oppressed, dumb like a lamb before the slaughter, cut off from the living, stricken for the sin of God's people, buried with the wicked, crushed with pain, anguished, poured out to death, counted among transgressors—and all of this despite never taking up violence and never uttering a single dishonest word (Isaiah 52:13–53:12).

As his vision unfolded, opposition to his message grew. Slaps and spitting, insults and beatings, were followed by the indignity of death. There was nothing *easy* about what the inspired prophet did. There is nothing easy about transformation.

Why? Because transformation requires transition, change, a new direction, and many of us—especially those who most need it—resist change. And change is exactly what the prophet demanded of his fellow Israelites in exile.

At a moment of vulnerability and pain, the prophet tells Israel that God is committed to the salvation of *every* nation, not just his own. It's time for Israel, exiled and exhausted though it be, to turn to the future with hope and openness even to its oppressors. God is the God of all nations, and God is about to bring salvation by the Persian ruler Cyrus, God's "messiah" (Isaiah 45:1).

This vision flies in the face of patriotism at the most difficult of times, when the nation's drive toward protectionism and isolation is at its height. These are a weary people, worn down by the destruction of Jerusalem, exhausted by the bullying of Babylon. The last thing they can imagine is a future when the descendants of Abraham and Sarah would include, on equal footing, the descendants of those who murdered their grandparents, when God would choose a powerful empire, an utter outsider, to liberate Israel.

Because his vision is so out of line with his countrymen and women, he meets with resistance, even a grueling death. He listened and learned. He brought a word of transformation. And he met brutal resistance. Transformation, the prophet shows us, no matter how rooted it is in preparation and how correct it may be, all too often generates opposition. If you are prepared to take this step, to become an engine of transformation, you must be ready as well for opposition. You must be ready to press ahead despite a heavy barrage of resistance.

THE CHURCH MOVED AND MOBILIZED

We've talked so far only about individuals. Still, while individuals often spearhead transformation, communities do as well. Just as often individuals and communities work together to bring a rich synergy that transforms our church and world. Just think of Bishop Wilberforce and the anti-slavery movement. Dorothy Day and the Catholic Worker Movement. Martin Luther King Jr. and the Civil Rights Movement. This is also true for transformation from a Native American perspective as the Reverend Anita Phillips explains: "Transformation is not a solitary endeavor. Transformation is an endless circle. Transformation impacts the individual and the network of relationships of that individual."

Transformation through a network of relationships characterized an inauspicious, almost inconspicuous small-town gathering that developed, in a surprisingly short span of time, into one of the largest and most influential groups of women ever to shape America.

In the winter of 1873 in Hillsboro, Ohio, a town of two thousand people that supported two distilleries and thirteen saloons, a group of women, mostly housewives, met in a Presbyterian church for a prayer meeting to combat the harmful impact of liquor sales on their homes, particularly on women and children who bore the brunt of domestic abuse fueled by alcohol. The consumption of liquor after the Civil War had risen to new heights, thanks to more efficient production and distribution techniques.

Prayer was soon joined by protest. The prayer meeting grew into a religious procession and crusade, as these women began to march and sing hymns on their way to demonstrations in front of the saloons of Hillsboro. The women compelled saloon owners to sign a pledge not to sell liquor. Several days later, in a nearby town, other women initiated a similar crusade. The movement swelled. In town after town, a prayer meeting and accompanying religious crusade, known as the "Woman's Crusade," spread quickly across the country, with over nine hundred groups at work by the summer of 1874.

The Woman's Crusade held meetings and staged marches. They also, on occasion, smashed beer barrels or poured the contents of liquor bottles into the street in front of the gathered crowds. Saloonkeepers throughout the nation met these actions with resistance. They began to harass the women by pouring buckets of dirty water on them, cursing them, or throwing rotten eggs at them. Some businessmen, more urbanely, took the women to court. Members of the Woman's Crusade, in turn, saw themselves as suffering for the sake of Christ, who himself had suffered. They sang hymns that captured the importance of suffering with Jesus:

Must Jesus bear the cross alone,
   and all the world go free?
No, there's a cross for everyone,
   and there's a cross for me.[8]

As Eliza Daniel "Mother" Stewart, a temperance worker in Ohio explained, "Thus we moved out, in great trembling, with bowed head, but with the eye of faith steadfastly fixed on the Cross of Calvary. . . . A holy inspiration filled our souls, and as the bell rang out its peals at the close of each prayer as a message of encouragement sent after us . . . we felt a sweet and holy joy come into our souls, a new, glad experience that buoyed us as if treading not upon the earth, but the air. Lo! We were walking with Jesus."[9]

If prayer turned to protest, protest turned political. A call went out to form a national temperance organization of women to fight the male-dominated liquor industry: "In the name of our Master [Jesus Christ]—in behalf of the thousands of women who suffer from this terrible evil—we call upon all to unite in an earnest, continued effort to hold the ground already won, and move onward together to a complete victory over the foes we fight."[10] From this call emerged, in November of 1874 in Cleveland, Ohio, a sisterhood of reform that formed the Woman's Christian Temperance Union (WCTU), which grew into the largest women's organization in the United States in the late 1800s, with a membership approaching two hundred thousand by the turn of the century.

With prayer, protest, and political clout came power. Under the nearly twenty-year presidency of Methodist lay leader, Frances Willard, the WCTU's agenda broadened to include other pivotal reforms, such as women's suffrage, women's health, women's dress reform, equal pay for women's equal work, the eradication of prostitution, an eight-hour workday, and women's equality in church polity. WCTU units in urban areas confronted issues of poverty and an unjust economic system, which heightened the deplorable living conditions for women and children. In a speech to the national WCTU in 1888, Willard encouraged women to study "causes rather than effects. For the more we study the causes, the more certainly we find that justice, not charity, must be the watchword of the future."[11]

This is the engine of transformation. Not just the two hundred thousand women who changed America forever, but the women in a town of two thousand who met to pray. Not just the massive and influential WCTU, which wielded power in Washington, DC, but women who marched to saloons, singing hymns in Hillsboro, Ohio. Not just the likes of Frances Willard and Eliza Stewart, but the unnamed souls who saw a problem and confronted it through prayer and protest. No start is too small, no prayer too meager, no group too insignificant to bring about transformation.

A COMMUNITY WITH A VISION FOR TRANSFORMATION

The history of the Christian church is one of salient moments of transformation alongside tragic moments of resistance. Early in the church's life we see a stellar example of a church community that provided the bedrock of the first great transformation in the history of Christianity. This community was not the church in Jerusalem. It wasn't the church in Rome. It was the church in Antioch, a lesser known city near the Mediterranean coast in modern-day Syria.[12] This community offers us, two thousand years later, a brilliant example of the threefold pattern: preparation-transformation-resistance.

PREPARATION
Here begins the first mission in the history of Christianity:

> Now in the church at Antioch there were prophets and teachers: Barnabas, Simeon who was called Niger, Lucius of Cyrene, Manaen a member of the court of Herod the ruler, and Saul. While they were worshiping the Lord and fasting, the Holy Spirit said, "Set apart for me Barnabas and Saul for the work to which I have called them." Then after fasting and praying they laid their hands on them and sent them off.
>
> So, being sent out by the Holy Spirit, they went down to Seleucia; and from there they sailed to Cyprus. (Acts 13:1–5)

Notice a few important things about the qualities and practices of this church, which made it the perfect launching pad for a barrier-breaking mission throughout the Mediterranean world.

A diverse leadership team. Antioch had a culturally and economically diverse leadership team. Simeon, "who was called Niger" (the word *Niger* in Greek is borrowed from a Latin word that means "black" or "dark-colored"), is probably from northern Africa. Lucius is also from northern Africa—modern-day Libya, to be exact. Manaen is—or was at one time—wealthy, and Herod Antipas's friend from youth. Compare him with Barnabas, who is not as well-heeled as he once was, since he sold some property and laid the proceeds at the apostles' feet to distribute (Acts 4:36-37). Saul, from Tarsus, a coastal city in Asia Minor, is a trained Pharisee.

A diverse leadership team makes this church the perfect launching pad for mission because it is itself a mission *in nuce*. In other words, Antioch was poised for the barrier-breaking transformation ahead because it had already broken barriers in its own community. If your community is mulling over a transformative activity, ask yourselves, "How are *we* already transformed in a way that makes us the perfect place for the transformation ahead?"

The right practices. The Spirit spoke to the Christians at Antioch "while they were worshiping the Lord and fasting" (13:2). Community disciplines provide the conditions for hearing a word of God that leads to transformation. It's that simple. A church involved in transformation should be a church committed to regular spiritual disciplines.

Notice something else, as well: these Christians didn't jump right on the command to ship Paul and Barnabas off somewhere. The Christians in Antioch returned to fasting—now with the addition of prayer—before laying their hands on Barnabas and Paul and sending them off. When they saw the way ahead, they worshiped and prayed and fasted even more. In Antioch, at least, a drastic shift, a fresh initiative, required preparation, which led to revelation, which led to transformation. Even after an inspired word came, the church returned to more prayer, not less.

See what's going on here? It's back to Chapter 1 for us!

A thirst for learning. Long before the Spirit spoke to this fasting-and-worshiping church, Barnabas and Saul (soon to be Paul) traveled to Antioch and "for an entire year they met with the church and taught a great many people, and it was in Antioch that the disciples were first called 'Christians'" (Acts 11:22–26). Intense learning for *an entire year*. What did they study? The Old Testament, of course: texts such as Isaiah 40–55, with its expansive passion for outsiders, aliens, and foreigners. Antioch wasn't a college or seminary, and your church doesn't need to be that either. However, if you want to be like Antioch, where the Holy Spirit spoke a word that would change the world—and themselves in the bargain—you need to develop a community where serious and sustained learning takes place. Yep, you guessed it: back to Chapter 2 we go to prepare ourselves for transformation!

We may wonder whether we do enough to transform our churches and our world. Are we stagnating because of inaction? Are we stale because of inactivity? Perhaps. But we learn from Antioch that the problem may lie elsewhere, in our *lack of readiness* to be people of transformation. Before we dive in head first, then, ask yourself and your community these questions.

- Do we embody in our community *already* the qualities we hope to cultivate in others?
- Do we live and breathe a vision of transformation drawn from scripture, from lifelong learning?
- Do we practice spiritual disciplines so regularly that we are in a place to receive God's guidance, maybe even through a revelation, as we move ahead?

TRANSFORMATION

We can still remember the maps on the walls of our Sunday school rooms. Priscilla was raised in Cincinnati and worshiped in a beautiful colonial church, complete with towering pillars, well-appointed and bright Sunday school rooms, and a well-organized regimen of mission trips. Jack worshiped in a small clapboard church tucked between a TV repair store and a donut shop, with basement Sunday school rooms that shared space with a belching oil furnace. Despite these differences, both of us learned about Paul's missionary journeys from maps tacked on the wall. They were confusing maps (just check the back of your Bible, and you'll see), in part because Paul covers so much of the same ground in later trips, in part because he also visits Jerusalem—not a mission trip exactly, but a journey included on the mission trip maps just, it seems to us, to confuse us.

Get mired in the details of these maps, and you'll miss the main point: Paul, Barnabas, and their companions broke all sorts of ethnic barriers, as they crisscrossed the Mediterranean Sea. The biggest barrier of all was the one that divided Jew from Gentile. Christianity, at the start, was part and parcel of Judaism. This was good, not least because Jews enjoyed privileges in the Roman Empire. Yet being Jewish meant, often enough, a sense of isolation. Take kosher food, for example. Many Jews could not eat with Gentile neighbors, and this situation created all sorts of mistrust, even hatred of Jews by their Gentile neighbors. Louis Feldman, an Orthodox Jewish scholar at Yeshiva University, made this point in a National Endowment for the Humanities Summer Seminar Jack participated in. Jews, he said, simply couldn't accept invitations to eat with neighbors. True enough, when the seminar group wanted to celebrate Louis's incredible mentoring, they had to arrange to take him to a deli that his rabbi could approve. (Admittedly, eating at a New York deli isn't a hardship, but the story makes the point about the isolation caused by eating only kosher food.)

Add to kosher laws all sorts of other commandments about not mixing certain kinds of cloths, farming in a certain way, marriage customs, and a slew of others, and you'll see that the expansion of Christianity into Gentile, non-Jewish communities was a transformation of epic proportions. In one community after another, Paul and Barnabas visited synagogue and town to tell people about Jesus. In one community after another, the good news brought Jew and Gentile together. Despite different clothes, different customs, even the different smells that different foods produce, people of different ethnic backgrounds worshiped, studied, and prayed together. Barriers came down.

We can see the residue of that transformation in the early Christian baptismal confession: "As many of you as were baptized into Christ have clothed yourselves with Christ. There is no longer Jew or Greek, there is no longer slave or free, there is no longer male and female; for all of you are one in Christ Jesus" (Galatians 3:27-28). What follows—Paul's commentary on this confession—is no less significant: "And if you belong to Christ, then you are

Abraham's offspring, heirs according to the promise" (3:29). The *you* in this commentary includes Gentiles, who, Paul knows, share the full inheritance with their Jewish brothers and sisters. Food, clothing, customs, economic status, ethnicity, gender—these don't matter a whiff for people clothed in Christ. Now *that* is a radical transformation.

We can see the ongoing power of that transformation in United Methodist Women. Josephine Beckwith (1908–2008), for example, gained a vision for racial transformation while growing up in an integrated neighborhood in Kansas City, Kansas, and later as a college student, when she was active in the Methodist Student Movement's interracial meetings in the 1930s. With the combined support of blacks and whites—her Methodist Church, the largest black Methodist church in Kansas City, Kansas, and Thelma Stevens, head of the Woman's Division of The Methodist Church at the time—she broke the color barrier in 1939 to enroll as a graduate student at the National College for Christian Workers, a training institute for women pursuing religious vocations run by the Women's Home Missionary Society. Her church supplied her with a scholarship to pay the school's fees, and Stevens challenged the Missouri state law that prevented blacks from enrolling at the school. The decision handed down by the state allowed Beckwith to enroll but not to live on campus. White students at National College, however, devised ways to circumvent the law by inviting her to stay overnight in their rooms in order for her to attend an evening or early morning class.

After graduation, Beckwith went on to work for the Woman's Division as director of several church-based community centers until, in 1958, she was appointed as director of the Bethlehem Community Center in Savannah, Georgia. In her 1959 annual report to the Woman's Division, Beckwith tied the work of the Bethlehem Center in Savannah to her vision to transform interracial cooperation: "The Community Center has been a demonstration of goodwill in our neighborhood. Some of the neighbors refuse to accept us but see daily people of a different skin color come into our building to lead a group, meet with a committee, or bring friends for a tour. A philosophy based on our Christian principles which include respect for those of a different race or creed must be a leavening force in this community."[13] Two years before she died at the age of one hundred, Beckwith told an interviewer that she approached her home missionary work as a means of "helping . . . people to understand each other" and to "really absorb what was going on in the world."[14] In doing so, she continued the legacy of the early church by challenging segregation and transforming relationships between blacks and whites.

RESISTANCE

Naturally, when a dramatic transformation happens, some people dig in their heels. This took place in the early days of the church, when the influx of non-Jewish believers in the early church raised an inevitable, impossible issue for some of Jesus' followers, who argued, "Unless you are circumcised according to the custom of Moses, you cannot be saved" (Acts 15:1). When they demanded a second time, "It is necessary for them [Gentiles] to be circumcised and ordered to keep the law of Moses" (15:5), the hair on Peter's neck stood up, and he protested with a declaration of his own experience:

> And God, who knows the human heart, testified to [the Gentiles] by giving them the Holy Spirit, just as he did to us; and in cleansing their hearts by faith he has made no distinction between them and us. Now therefore why are you putting God to the test by placing on the neck of the disciples a yoke that neither our ancestors nor we have been able to bear? On the contrary, we believe that we will be saved through the grace of the Lord Jesus, just as they will. (15:8–11)

Paul and Barnabas joined the fray and narrated their own experience "of all the signs and wonders that God had done through them among the Gentiles" (15:12).

The battle lines were now drawn. Some of Jesus' followers were saying something like, "Circumcise the Gentiles who believe in Jesus because it's required by Torah!" Peter, Paul, and Barnabas responded, "Don't circumcise the Gentiles, who have received the Holy Spirit without circumcision!" They couldn't agree with their brothers about circumcision because they saw first-hand that Gentiles received the Holy Spirit without first being circumcised.

An explosion rattled the church in Antioch: "And after Paul and Barnabas had no small dissension and debate with them [the believers who championed circumcision], Paul and Barnabas and some of the others were appointed to go up to Jerusalem to discuss this question with the apostles and the elders" (Acts 15:2). The word *dissension* (*stasis*) is later used in Acts to describe Ephesian riots (19:40; *rioting* in NRSV) and a rigid division between Pharisees and Sadducees, which turned so violent that "the tribune, fearing that they would tear Paul to pieces, ordered the soldiers to go down, take him by force, and bring him into the barracks" (23:7, 10). This "no small dissension" in Antioch, which pitted Peter and Paul against the Pharisaic followers of Jesus, therefore, was not civil debate. It was aggressive and vicious conflict.

Transformation, yet again, evoked resistance—in this case, violent resistance. Resistance that not even the good people of the church in Antioch could resolve, so they passed it along to Jerusalem, where James, the leader in Jerusalem, sided (more or less) with Peter, Paul, and Barnabas by agreeing that God looked favorably upon the Gentiles (Acts 15:14). He then turned to scripture—no surprise here; he had been doing his own study of the prophets—to support this decision, citing Amos 9:11-12, followed by a snippet from Isaiah 45:21. The point he made, on the basis of scripture, was that the nations, the Gentiles, are part of God's rebuilding of Israel.

Conflict avoided. Schism averted. Yet it wasn't easy. A well-prepared church in Antioch had launched a barrier-breaking transformation, which was met with violent resistance. Such, often enough, is the fate of transformation when it is, as it was at Antioch, well-conceived and executed.

BEEKEEPING AND TRANSFORMATION

Transformation throughout the centuries has taken many forms, some of them surprising, many of them unlikely. In our day, for example, "in the West Bank villages of Bil'in and Nil'in, just outside of Ramallah, 30 women have used the power of honey to keep their communities—and their livelihoods—cohesive and resolute."[15] The Palestine beekeeping project, which identifies and trains women in beekeeping and honey-related uses and marketing, is making a significant impact on women, families, and the Palestinian community. The project was launched and continues to be maintained thanks to a three-way affiliation between the Grassroots International's Women's Empowerment Project, the Union of Agricultural Work Committees (UAWC)-Palestine, and United Methodist Women. This beekeeping project is a model of the pattern, preparation-transformation-resistance.

PREPARATION

The organizers began, in the first place, by asking which agricultural project would be viable. After careful consideration, they decided on beekeeping because the West Bank's vegetation produces nectar for the bees, and honey is a highly sought-after commodity. Beekeeping seemed the perfect project for this area in the West Bank. Next came the need to select beekeepers. The organizers chose trainees on the basis of four factors: "their knowledge, previous experience in target areas, leadership skills and volunteer involvement." These women were trained thoroughly in a range of skills, from beekeeping to marketing. To ensure success, the organizers provided these select women with "agricultural resources, vocational training and technical assistance throughout the entire project."[16]

TRANSFORMATION

A host of women have been transformed by being able to provide income for their families, as well as honing their leadership skills. "Strengthening the women's leadership and employment skills through the cooperative experience also empowers women more than emergency or relief projects."[17] Transformation extends beyond individual women, their families, and villages. Ripples of hope and economic well-being reach throughout the Palestinian community, thanks to the decision to adopt a collective approach to beekeeping, in which farmers work cooperatively to grow, harvest, and market bees and honey. A web of communication, economic strength, and hopefulness is emerging from a surprising place: beehives on the West Bank.

RESISTANCE

Organizers chose to place beehives near the Israeli Separation Wall, which is maintained by Israeli forces, even though the International Court of Justice declared the Wall contrary to international law. Since two-thirds of the villages' farmland was confiscated with the building of the Separation Wall, organizers placed the hives near the wall on purpose, in order to maintain a hold on the land so that it won't be taken over by Israeli forces. "We have to protect our land," explained Union of Agricultural Work Committees bee-keeper Salwa Hasan, "and putting these beehives here is how we do it. We are developing ourselves, and we are challenging the occupation."[18] Challenge, of course, meets with resistance. Heavy militarization around the Wall has caused serious damage to the bees. Bees have become sick or died due to Israeli tear gas unleashed in the crackdown against demonstrators.

The Palestinian beekeeping project is a stellar example of the synergy that connects preparation, transformation, and resistance. It is an example as well of a meaningful connection between individual and community effort. It is also an example of how well secular and Christian organizations can work together in careful preparation, effective grassroots transformation, and standing together against a wall of resistance.

PRAY, LEARN, MENTOR, TRANSFORM

United Methodist Women, by the title of this spiritual growth study, has suggested that the question, "How is it with your soul?" which was pivotal to early Methodists who participated in weekly class meetings, is a question for our day as well. This is not a question that can be answered well if it is answered passively. Think back to the questions John Wesley raised to assess the state of the soul:

- Have you carefully abstained from doing evil?
- Have you zealously maintained good works?
- Have you constantly attended on all the ordinances of God?[19]

These are active questions that assume a posture of engagement—adverbs and verbs like "carefully abstain," "zealously maintain," and "constantly attend."

In keeping with Wesley's focus on verbs, we have chosen four for this spiritual growth study: *pray, learn, mentor, transform.* Now, in closing, let's invest these verbs with the tenor of John Wesley's ardor and ask them directly:

- Will you regularly create time and space to pray?
- Will you carefully learn Jesus through the study of scripture?
- Will you wisely mentor someone, whether familiar or unexpected?
- Will you zealously transform pockets of injustice?

Together, these questions frame a powerful mandate, a great commission, one for which Jesus inspires—inbreathes—us, just as he did in the upper room: "'As the Father has sent me, so I send you.' When he had said this, he breathed into them and said to them, 'Receive the Holy Spirit'" (John 20:21-22).

Endnotes

INTRODUCTION

1 John H. Wigger, *Taking Heaven by Storm: Methodism and the Rise of Popular Christianity in America* (Chicago, IL: University of Illinois Press, 2001), 81.

2 Ibid.

3 "Rules of the Band Societies, Drawn up Dec. 25, 1738," in *The Works of John Wesley*, vol. 9, The *Methodist Societies: History, Nature, and Design*, Rupert E. Davies, ed. (Nashville, TN: Abingdon Press, 1989), 77.

4 "Directions given to the Band Societies, Dec. 25, 1744," in Davies, *The Works of John Wesley*, vol. 9, *The Methodist Societies: History, Nature, and Design*, 79.

5 Wigger, *Taking Heaven by Storm*, 85.

6 Randy L. Maddox, "Reclaiming Holistic Salvation," *Circuit Rider* (May/June 2003): 15.

CHAPTER 1: PRAY

1 "Thou Hidden Love of God," Gerhard Tersteegen, translated by John Wesley, *The United Methodist Hymnal* (Nashville, TN: The United Methodist Publishing House, 1989), #414, stanza 5.

2 Macrina Wiederkehr, *Seven Sacred Pauses: Living Mindfully Through the Hours of the Day* (Notre Dame, IN: Sorin Books, 2008), 95.

3 Charles Wallace, Jr., ed., *Susanna Wesley: The Complete Writings* (New York: Oxford University Press, 1997), 50.

4 Ibid., 208.

5 Christine Valters Paintner and Lucy Wynkoop, *Lectio Divina: Contemplative Awakening and Awareness* (New York: Paulist Press, 2008), 12.

6 Ibid., 26.

7 See Roy DeLeon, *Praying With the Body: Bringing the Psalms to Life* (Brewster, MA: Paraclete Press, 2009).

8 Su Yon Pak, Unzu Lee, Jung Ha Kim, and Myung Ji Cho, *Singing the Lord's Song in a New Land: Korean American Practices of Faith* (Louisville, KY: Westminster John Knox, 2005), 36.

CHAPTER 2: LEARN

1 *Sermons on Several Occasions*, Vol. 1, (1746), Preface, §5, *The Bicentennial Edition of The Works of John Wesley* (Nashville, TN: Abingdon Press, 1984), 1:104-5.

2 Eugene Peterson, *Eat This Book: A Conversation in the Art of Spiritual Reading* (Grand Rapids, MI: Eerdmans, 2006), 58.

3 To learn more about Antioch as a locus of learning, see Jack Levison, *Fresh Air: The Holy Spirit for an Inspired Life* (Brewster, MA: Paraclete, 2012), 150-53.

4   Lucy Rider Meyer, *Deaconesses: Biblical, Early Church, European, American* (Chicago, IL: The Message Publishing Company, 1889), 90.

5   Catherine M. Prelinger and Rosemary Skinner Keller, "The Function of Female Bonding: The Restored Diaconessate of the Nineteenth Century" in *Women in New Worlds*, Volume II, eds. Rosemary Skinner Keller, Louise L. Queen, and Hilah F. Thomas (Nashville, TN: Abingdon, 1982), 326.

6   Isabelle Horton, *High Adventure: Life of Lucy Rider Meyer* (New York: The Methodist Book Concern, 1928), 139.

7   Quoted in Randy L. Maddox, "The Rule of Christian Faith, Practice, and Hope"; *Methodist Review*, Vol. 3 (2011), 33. http://www.methodistreview.org/index.php/mr/article/view/45/68.

8   Burton H. Throckmorton, *Gospel Parallels: A Comparison of the Synoptic Gospels, New Revised Standard Version, 5th revised edition* (Nashville, TN: Thomas Nelson, 1992).

9   Randy Maddox, 19.

10 Ibid., 27.

11 John R. (Jack) Levison and Priscilla Pope-Levison, eds. *Return to Babel: Global Perspectives on the Bible* (Louisville, KY: Westminster John Knox, 1999), 125-26.

12 Ibid., 131-32.

13 Peterson, *Eat This Book*, 55.

14 Eugene Peterson, *A Long Obedience in the Same Direction: Discipleship in an Instant Society* (Downers Grove, IL: InterVarsity Press, 2000), 204.

15 Paintner and Wynkoop, *Lectio Divina*, 2.

16 Joan Chittister, *The Rule of Benedict: A Spirituality for the 21st Century* (New York: Crossroad, 2010), 3.

17 Peterson, *Eat This Book*, 92.

18 Paintner and Wynkoop, *Lectio Divina*, 4.

CHAPTER 3: MENTOR

1   Donald Demaray, ed., *Devotions and Prayers of John Wesley* (Grand Rapids, MI: Baker Book House, 1959), 107.

2   Lucy Rider Meyer, *Deaconesses: Biblical, Early Church, European, American* (Chicago, IL: The Message Publishing Company, 1889), 86.

3   Isabelle Horton, *High Adventure: Life of Lucy Rider Meyer* (New York: The Methodist Book Concern, 1928), 204.

4   John A. Newton, *Susanna Wesley and the Puritan Tradition in Methodism*, 2nd ed. (London: Epworth Press, 2002), 105.

5   Ibid., 122.

6   Ibid.

7   Ibid., 125.

8   Harold E. Raser, *Phoebe Palmer: Her Life and Thought (Studies in Women and Religion)*, vol. 22 (Lewiston, NY: Edwin Mellen, 1987), 26.

9   Priscilla Pope-Levison, *Turn the Pulpit Loose: Two Centuries of American Women Evangelists* (New York: Palgrave Macmillan, 2004), 62-63.

10 Katie Geneva Cannon, "Surviving the Blight," in Letty Russell, et. al., *Inheriting Our Mothers' Gardens: Feminist Theology in Third World Perspective* (Louisville, KY: Westminster John Knox Press, 1988), 88.

11 William Yoo, "Crossing Racial, Religious, and National Boundaries: The Impact of a Friendship between American and Korean Women from North Georgia to South Korea, 1948-1965," Paper delivered at the American Academy of Religion Meeting, Chicago, Illinois, November 2012.

12 Ibid.

13 Ibid.

14 Horton, *High Adventure*, 209.

15 Russell E. Richey, "The Formation of American Methodism: The Chesapeake Refraction of Wesleyanism," in *Methodism and the Shaping of American Culture,* Nathan O. Hatch and John H. Wigger, eds. (Nashville, TN: Kingswood Books, Abingdon Press, 2001), 216-17.

CHAPTER 4: TRANSFORM

1 "Christ, from Whom All Blessings Flow," Charles Wesley, *The United Methodist Hymnal* (Nashville, TN: The United Methodist Publishing House, 1989), #550, stanzas 5 and 6.

2 Emilie M. Townes, "Because God Gave Her Vision: The Religious Impulse of Ida B. Wells-Barnett," in Rosemary Skinner Keller, *Spirituality & Social Responsibility: Vocational Vision of Women in The United Methodist Tradition* (Nashville, TN: Abingdon Press, 1993), 156 57.

3 Ibid., 155.

4 Ibid., 146.

5 Ibid., 163.

6 Ibid., 149.

7 We know this for sure. It's not just in our Bibles, in Hebrew (Ezra 1:2-4), the language of Israel, and Aramaic, the language of Persia (Ezra 6:3-5).

8 "Must Jesus Bear the Cross Alone," Thomas Shepherd, *The United Methodist Hymnal* (Nashville, TN: The United Methodist Publishing House, 1989), #424, stanza 1.

9 Carolyn DeSwarte Gifford, "Women in Social Reform Movements," in *Women & Religion in America: Volume 1, The Nineteenth Century, A Documentary History,* Rosemary Radford Ruether and Rosemary Skinner Keller, eds. (San Francisco: Harper & Row, 1981), 324.

10 Carolyn DeSwarte Gifford, "Nineteenth- and Twentieth-Century Protestant Social Reform Movements in the United States," in *Encyclopedia of Women and Religion in North America,* Rosemary Skinner Keller and Rosemary Radford Ruether, eds. (Bloomington, IN: Indiana University Press, 2006), III:1028.

11 Ibid.

12 For more on the remarkable qualities of Antioch, see Levison, *Fresh Air*, 153-65.

13 Mary K. Schueneman, "A Leavening Force: African American Women and Christian Mission in the Civil Rights Era," *Church History* 81:4 (December 2012): 893-94.

14 Ibid., 901.

15 "The Women's Empowerment Project," http://new.gbgm-umc.org/umw/resources/articles/item/index.cfm?id=1006.

16 Ibid.

17 Ibid.

18 "Up Against the Wall: Beehives of Resistance and Self-Determination," Sara Mersha, http://www.grassrootsonline.org/news/blog/women-beekeeping-collectives-nurture-life-and-resistance-shadow-wall.

19 "Directions given to the Band Societies, Dec. 25, 1744," in Davies, *The Works of John Wesley*, vol. 9, *The Methodist Societies: History, Nature, and Design*, 79.

Bibliography

Cannon, Katie Geneva. "Surviving the Blight." In *Inheriting Our Mothers' Gardens: Feminist Theology in Third World Perspective*, ed. Letty Russell, et. al., 75-90. Louisville, KY: Westminster John Knox Press, 1988.

Chittister, Joan. *The Rule of Benedict: A Spirituality for the 21ˢᵗ Century*. New York: Crossroad, 2010.

Davies, Rupert E., ed. *The Works of John Wesley*, vol. 9, *The Methodist Societies: History, Nature, and Design*. Nashville, TN: Abingdon Press, 1989.

DeLeon, Roy. *Praying With the Body: Bringing the Psalms to Life*. Brewster, MA: Paraclete Press, 2009.

Demaray, Donald, ed. *Devotions and Prayers of John Wesley*. Grand Rapids, MI: Baker Book House, 1959.

Gifford, Carolyn DeSwarte. "Nineteenth- and Twentieth-Century Protestant Social Reform Movements in the United States." In *Encyclopedia of Women and Religion in North America,* eds. Rosemary Skinner Keller and Rosemary Radford Ruether, III:1021-38. Bloomington, IN: Indiana University Press, 2006.

_____. "Women in Social Reform Movements." In *Women & Religion in America*: Volume 1, *The Nineteenth Century, A Documentary History,* eds. Rosemary Radford Ruether and Rosemary Skinner Keller, 294-340. San Francisco: Harper & Row, 1981.

Horton, Isabelle. *High Adventure: Life of Lucy Rider Meyer*. New York: The Methodist Book Concern, 1928.

Levison, Jack. *Fresh Air: The Holy Spirit for an Inspired Life.* Brewster, MA: Paraclete Press, 2012.

Levison, John R. and Priscilla Pope-Levison, eds. *Return to Babel: Global Perspectives on the Bible.* Louisville, KY: Westminster John Knox, 1999.

Maddox, Randy. "Reclaiming Holistic Salvation." *Circuit Rider* (May/June 2003): 14-15.

_____. "The Rule of Christian Faith, Practice and Hope: John Wesley on the Bible." *Methodist Review* 3 (2011): 1-35. http://www.methodistreview .org/index.php/mr/article/view/45/68.

Mersha, Sara. "Up Against the Wall: Beehives of Resistance and Self-Determination." http://www.grassrootsonline.org/news/blog/women-beekeeping -collectives-nurture-life-and-resistance-shadow-wall.

Meyer, Lucy Rider. *Deaconesses: Biblical, Early Church, European, American.* Chicago, IL: The Message Publishing Company, 1889.

Newton, John A. *Susanna Wesley and the Puritan Tradition in Methodism,* 2nd ed. London: Epworth Press, 2002.

Paintner, Christine Valters and Lucy Wynkoop. *Lectio Divina: Contemplative Awakening and Awareness.* New York: Paulist Press, 2008.

Pak, Su Yon, Unzu Lee, Jung Ha Kim, and Myung Ji Cho, eds. *Singing the Lord's Song in a New Land: Korean American Practices of Faith.* Louisville, KY: Westminster John Knox, 2005.

Peterson, Eugene. *Eat This Book: A Conversation in the Art of Spiritual Reading.* Grand Rapids, MI: Eerdmans, 2006.

_____. *A Long Obedience in the Same Direction: Discipleship in an Instant Society.* Downers Grove, IL: InterVarsity Press, 2000.

Pope-Levison, Priscilla. *Turn the Pulpit Loose: Two Centuries of American Women Evangelists.* New York: Palgrave Macmillan, 2004.

Prelinger, Catherine M. and Rosemary Skinner Keller. "The Function of Female Bonding: The Restored Diaconessate of the Nineteenth Century." In *Women in New Worlds,* Volume II, eds. Rosemary Skinner Keller, Louise L. Queen, and Hilah F. Thomas, 318-37. Nashville, TN: Abingdon Press, 1982.

Raser, Harold E. *Phoebe Palmer: Her Life and Thought. Studies in Women and Religion,* vol. 22. Lewiston, NY: Edwin Mellen Press, 1987.

Richey, Russell E. "The Formation of American Methodism: The Chesapeake Refraction of Wesleyanism." In *Methodism and the Shaping of American Culture,* eds. Nathan O. Hatch and John H. Wigger, 197-222. Nashville, TN: Kingswood Books, Abingdon Press, 2001.

Schueneman, Mary K. "A Leavening Force: African American Women and Christian Mission in the Civil Rights Era." *Church History* 81:4 (December 2012): 873-902.

Sermons on Several Occasions, Vol. 1, (1746), *The Bicentennial Edition of The Works of John Wesley.* Nashville, TN: Abingdon Press, 1984.

Throckmorton, Burton H. *Gospel Parallels: A Comparison of the Synoptic Gospels, New Revised Standard Version, 5th revised edition.* Nashville, TN: Thomas Nelson Press, 1992.

Townes, Emilie M. "Because God Gave Her Vision: The Religious Impulse of Ida B. Wells-Barnett." In *Spirituality & Social Responsibility: Vocational Vision of Women in The United Methodist Tradition,* ed. Rosemary Skinner Keller, 139-63. Nashville, TN: Abingdon Press, 1993.

Wallace, Charles, Jr., ed. *Susanna Wesley: The Complete Writings*. New York: Oxford University Press, 1997.

Wiederkehr, Macrina. *Seven Sacred Pauses: Living Mindfully Through the Hours of the Day*. Notre Dame, IN: Sorin Books, 2008.

Wigger, John H. *Taking Heaven by Storm: Methodism and the Rise of Popular Christianity in America*. Chicago, IL: University of Illinois Press, 2001.

"The Women's Empowerment Project." http://new.gbgm-umc.org/umw/re sources/articles/item/index.cfm?id=1006.

Yoo, William. "Crossing Racial, Religious, and National Boundaries: The Impact of a Friendship between American and Korean Women from North Georgia to South Korea, 1948-1965." Paper delivered at the American Academy of Religion Meeting, Chicago, Illinois, November 2012.

About the Authors

Priscilla Pope-Levison (@profppl; http://myhome.spu.edu/popep/) came to the Pacific Northwest twelve years ago for a faculty appointment as Professor of Theology and Assistant Director of Women's Studies at Seattle Pacific University, and she has fallen in love with the region. Her interdisciplinary publications combine Theology, Gender Studies, Church History, and Mission and Evangelism. She recently completed her sixth book, *Building the Old Time Religion: Women Evangelists in the Progressive Era* (NYU Press, 2014). She has also authored, *Turn the Pulpit Loose: Two Centuries of American Women Evangelists* and *Evangelization from a Liberation Perspective.* With her spouse of more than thirty years, Jack Levison, she has published *Sex, Gender, and Christianity*; *Jesus in Global Contexts*; and *Return to Babel: Global Perspectives on the Bible.* Pope-Levison hosted "Jesus in the Gospels" for the Second Generation Series of DISCIPLE Bible Study. She is an ordained United Methodist minister and has served as a local church pastor and as a college chaplain.

Called a "brilliant and spirited theologian" by author Phyllis Tickle, Jack Levison is a featured blogger for *The Huffington Post* (http://www.huffing tonpost.com/jack-levison/) and a regular contributor to Patheos (http://www.patheos.com/blogs/spiritchatter/), the world's largest independent site for conversations on religion. Jack is an internationally recognized scholar, whose books have received wide acclaim. Eugene Peterson, author of *The Message,* considers him "the most competent scholar and clearest writer on the Holy Spirit that I have known." Jack has received grants from the National Humanities Center, the Lilly Fellows Program, the Louisville Institute, the Alexander von Humboldt Foundation, the Rotary Foundation, the International Catacomb Society, and the National Endowment for the Humanities. He directs an international research project, The Historical Roots of the Holy Spirit, and is founding editor of a new book series, *Ekstasis: Religious Experience from Antiquity to the Middle Ages.* He currently serves as president of the Pacific Northwest Region of the American Academy of Religion and Society of Biblical Literature. Raised on Long Island, New York, Jack attended Wheaton College, Cambridge University, and Duke University.

How Is It with Your Soul?

Participant's Guide by Faye Wilson

This Is *Your* Guide

The purpose for this section of the book is to assist you—either as part of a class or as an individual—to answer the question (perhaps anew or for the first time),

"How is it with your soul?"

This question is a key part of our Wesleyan heritage and our United Methodist Church history. It is a question that summons us to live more holy, to live more lovingly, and to give more sacrificially as a result of responding to the great invitation—to be a disciple of Jesus Christ.

The chapters in this study book are organized around four life-changing verbs: Pray, Learn, Mentor, and Transform. These words call us to action—individually and collectively.

- When we **pray,** we submit ourselves to God's will again and again. We lay the needs of our family, our community, even our world before the throne of grace.
- As we **learn**, we become keenly (and truthfully) aware of the complexity of life's challenges and successes that are part of the lives of people we know and have never met. We learn so we can act mindfully and lovingly.
- When we **mentor**, we give back to someone what has been given us. We pledge to walk alongside of others and be their guide and support.
- And when we do all of these things, we are making a commitment to **transform**—to be changed and become the change that the world needs so desperately.

If you are experiencing this study in a group setting (Mission u, perhaps), you will also participate in the Wesleyan model of accountability and discipleship known as the class meeting, which you will learn about in Session 1. As part of being in the group setting, you will also commit to honoring a code of confidentiality and learning about sharing with others in the manner of holy conferencing.

Generally, each session will have common elements. Depending upon your leader and the time available, some may be eliminated or rearranged, which is fine. The usual order, which you will see reflected in this Participant's Guide, begins with the Gathering Worship and then a Meet n' Greet. The session then moves into study and reflection with the Text and Context, Class Meeting, and Respond and Reflect portions. Finally, there is a Call to Action, followed by Closing Worship, and Assignments.

FOR LEADERS

If you are planning to teach this course in a group setting, be sure to download the free online Leader's Guide from www.unitedmethodist women.org. The Leader's Guide has four sessions (based on the four key words: pray, learn, mentor, and transform). It includes a variety of exercises to build community and encourage reflection.

Your study leader will be your guide; this book will make following along and participating easier. For example, words to be spoken in unison are in bold. Some places also issue an invitation to you to volunteer in specific ways. Please do! Make this your study.

If you are experiencing this study as an individual, you will see that you can easily adapt most of the group activities to guide your personal reflection and spiritual growth. Some adaptations are already provided for you. In addition to your own study and thoughtfulness, you may also wish to speak with friends and loved ones who are on similar journeys. With them you can share your observations, questions, and ideas and benefit from theirs.

Your Journal

The tradition of writing in a journal or diary goes way back in Methodist history. Philip F. Hardt, in researching the history of John Street United Methodist Church in New York City, found in the rare books room of the New York Public Library some original diaries of individual members of classes along with several class lists.[1]

As class members and individuals, you are encouraged to keep a journal or diary during your Mission u experience or your personal study. You may want to create one or use a notebook you've already started. You may take time at the end of the first class to create it, or you can make it at home. Your study leader may even have materials you can use—such as construction paper, glitter, glue, plain paper, and markers—to make your diary, which will be a memento for this period of study.

At designated times in the session or soon after it, take a few quiet moments to review what you have read, thought, talked about; to record your ideas, challenges, and plans. Items in your journal might also include names of members of the class, prayer concerns, significant scriptures, books that you have read or want to read, new information from the class, personal challenges, areas for growth.

Code of Confidentiality and Conduct[2]

(This is a sample; each class, with the facilitator, may develop its own.)
Every class member is valued.
Everyone has a right to speak.
No one is to use her or his voice or actions to hurt another.
No one is to dismiss the words and concerns of another classmate.
What is said in class remains in class.
No one's story shall be shared without that person's permission.
Provide empathy and care where appropriate.
Listen. Speak. Listen. Pray

Recommendations for Holy Conferencing[3]

- Every person is a child of God. Always speak respectfully. One can disagree without being disagreeable.
- As you patiently listen and observe the behavior of others, be open to the possibility that God can change the views of any or all parties in the discussion.
- Listen patiently before formulating responses.
- Strive to understand the experience out of which others have arrived at their views.
- Be careful in how you express personal offense at differing opinions. Otherwise, dialogue may be inhibited.
- Accurately reflect the views of others when speaking. This is especially important when you disagree with that position.
- Avoid using inflammatory words, derogatory names, or an excited and angry voice.
- Avoid making generalizations about individuals and groups. Make your point with specific evidence and examples.
- Make use of facilitators and mediators.
- Remember that people are defined, ultimately, by their relationship with God—not by the flaws we discover, or think we discover, in their views and actions.

Session 1: Pray

WELCOME!

The goal of Session 1 is to renew our commitment to pray for one another and for the world, a key principle of discipleship.

OBJECTIVES FOR THE SESSION

- To gain a portrait of prayer through recalling Hannah's prayer story
- To renew our commitment to prayer as a privilege not a chore or duty
- To revive our spiritual covenant with God and each other by connecting with John Wesley's class system model

MEMORY QUOTE

Work on memorizing this statement, which is based on Colossians 4:2-3. It is the same for each session to facilitate your memorization and internalization.

Devote yourselves to prayer, keeping alert in it with thanksgiving. At the same time pray for us as well. Watch and pray!

GATHERING WORSHIP

Song/Hymn

"Precious Lord, Take My Hand," *United Methodist Hymnal, #474*

Scripture

1 Samuel 1:1-15

Prayer (unison)

God, we come today to present our minds to be transformed by the power of your Word in scripture and in the lives of each other. We present ourselves so that you may speak to our inmost souls and say, "I am thy love, thy God, thy all." We are your children. We put our hope and our trust in you. Amen.

Litany

One Voice (volunteer): Gracious God, we open our hearts to you. Jesus, our Teacher, teach us to pray as you taught your disciples.

Many Voices: **Gracious God, we are a praying people.**

One Voice: You said that if your people who are called by your name would humble themselves and pray and seek your face, and turn from their wicked ways, you would hear them, forgive their sins, and heal their land. (See 2 Chronicles 7:14.)

Many Voices: **Gracious God, we are a praying people.**

One Voice: We lift our voices to ask for your guidance and direction. Speak to our hearts, Lord. We long for a word from you so that we may do the work to which you've called us.

All Voices: **Gracious God, teach us to pray. Teach us to love. Teach us to act according to your will, O loving God, for we *are* a praying people.**

Song/Hymn: "Lord, Listen to Your Children Praying," *The Faith We Sing,* #2193

MEET 'N' GREET

TEXT AND CONTEXT

Read Chapter 1. Individually identify

- Ten things that stand out in the text
- Two ideas you would like to know more about
- Five things that evoke memories in your life

If you are in a group setting, discuss these learnings and reflections in small groups in preparation for sharing with the entire class.

CLASS MEETING

Learn About the Wesley Class Meeting

John Wesley created three basic organizations for the nurture of people who wanted a closer walk with God: local societies, bands, and classes.

The first of the structures, the **local societies,** most mirrors what we might refer to as our churches. In this basic organizational unit, society members met weekly to pray and support one another in the Christian life.

A second structure was that of the **bands**. These were small groups, organized by gender, age, and marital status. Research indicates that in these groups the discussion focused on examining the spiritual health of the societies to see if people were maintaining their Christian walk.

The third structure is known as the **class meeting**. These were support-type groups of ten to twelve persons in which people practiced accountability for their faith walk and for one another. It is in this small group where members individually answered the question, How is it with your soul? There were actually three questions that answered this main one:

1. Have you carefully abstained from doing evil?
2. Have you zealously maintained good works?
3. Have you constantly attended on all the ordinances of God?

Answering these questions, as well as recounting acts of piety and acts of mercy, brought strength to those who participated. The practice also helped deepen the commitment of those who were deciding whether this way of life was for them. John Wesley believed that this group helped people to go on to "perfection."

Sin Ho Kim said that John Wesley wanted the members of the societies to "watch over and help each other" so they would not "[fall] away from faith and holiness." Salvation, fellowship, and discipleship were emphasized. Philip F. Hardt describes the class meeting structure as the "soul of Methodism."[1] He advocates that churches use this historical model to enhance unity, strengthen leadership, and gain new members.

Experience the Class Meeting (group)

1. Select a name for the class. *(Classes are requested to name themselves using the name of a biblical woman such as Hannah, Dorcas, Ruth, Naomi, or that of a key woman in Methodism/United Methodist Women such as Susanna Wesley, Sarah Crosby, Barbara Heck, Sojourner Truth, Lucy Rider Meyer, Phoebe Palmer, Fanny Crosby, Isabella Thoburn, Clara Swain, Anna Howard Shaw, Frances Willard, Thelma Stevenson, Mai Gray, Theressa Hoover.)*
2. Name a class leader (may be appointed by study leader) and a class recorder.
3. Introduce yourselves (name, conference/church, and one gift you use in your church).
4. Briefly answer the questions (one- to two-minute responses): How is it with your soul? For whom or what have you prayed this week?
5. Make notes about the prayer concerns you have just heard.
6. Close with a benediction:
   May the words of my mouth and the meditation of my heart be acceptable in God's sight. Amen.

Class Meeting (individual)

Answer the questions (aloud or write in a journal):

- How is it with your soul?
- For whom or what have you prayed this week?

Also, consider answering these questions:

- Do you [or your church community] have a regular PRACTICE of prayer (for example, every morning, at the church)?
- Do you have a PLACE of prayer (perhaps at the beach, in a church building, a special place set aside in your home)?
- Do you have a PATTERN for prayer (such as a Bible reading or liturgy, or are your prayers extemporaneous)?

RESPOND AND REFLECT

Take a few quiet moments to review what you have read or heard and your thoughts. Write in your diary about the importance of prayer in your life both when you were prayed for and when you prayed for someone. You may also include scripture that is significant to you, reflections or questions from your reading, a prayer that you write or one that has special meaning for you, and so forth. Be creative and include poetry, artwork, magazine photos, or pictures of family and friends.

CALL TO ACTION

CLOSING WORSHIP

Song/Hymn

"Sweet Hour of Prayer," *United Methodist Hymnal*, #496; "Lord, Listen to Your Children Praying," *The Faith We Sing*, #2193; or "All I Need Is You," *The Faith We Sing*, #2080

Tong-sung ki-do **Prayer (group):** Kneel at your chairs or in an open space (if able) in the posture of Korean Christians. If you do not choose to or cannot kneel, remain seated and pound fist on table or desk. Someone might use a cane to thump the floor. Remember, everyone prays at once.

Tong-sung ki-do **Prayer (individual):** This style of prayer is also called a shout-out prayer. So rather than simply reading it, allow yourself to shout the words and do the motions, including the pounding. Let yourself go fully into this whole-body prayer.

Pray

> **Jooyeo – Jooyeo – Jooyeo!** [JOO-ee-oh]
> *[pound on floor or table three times, then raise hands upward]*
>
> **Dear God, hear our cries. Jooyeo – Jooyeo – Jooyeo!**
> *[pound on floor or table three times, then raise hands upward]*
>
> **Can't you see the needs of your people? Hear us, we pray, and come speedily to help us. Jooyeo – Jooyeo – Jooyeo!**
> *[pound on floor or table three times, then raise hands upward]*
>
> **We lift our hearts and voices to you. Deepen within us a desire to be in fellowship with you or share your love in the world. Jooyeo – Jooyeo – Jooyeo!**
> *[pound on floor or table three times, then raise hands upward]*
>
> **In Jesus' name we pray, Amen.**

Return to your seat.

Closing
Read aloud the names of persons and mission projects from the Prayer Calendar.

Experience a moment of silence and then join in this recommitment:

Lord, we go forth this day, renewed in our desire to pray. We will pray so that the world will be blessed. We will pray so that others may come to know you. Amen.

ASSIGNMENTS

Read Chapter 2. Write down ten things that stand out for you.

If your church has a class meeting type system, please let your leader know. Volunteer to come to Session 2 prepared to share the value of the class meeting system with the group.

Session 2: Learn

WELCOME!

The goal of Session 2 is to renew our commitment to learning by understanding the role of study in the spreading of the gospel in the disciples' time as well as in the beginning of The United Methodist Church.

OBJECTIVES FOR THE SESSION

- To rededicate ourselves to study and action
- To understand the intense learning process that accompanied the spread of the gospel in the disciples' time as well as in the early days of Methodism
- To continue our spiritual covenant with God and each other by using the Wesley Class Meeting model

MEMORY QUOTE

[Based on Colossians 4:2-3]

Devote yourselves to prayer, keeping alert in it with thanksgiving. At the same time pray for us as well. Watch and pray!

GATHERING WORSHIP

Song/Hymn

"Praise the Source of Faith and Learning," *The Faith We Sing*, #2004; or "Tell Me the Stories of Jesus," *United Methodist Hymnal*, #277

Scripture
Psalm 119:10-16

Prayer (volunteer)

Litany
One Voice (volunteer): Lord, teach us to hide your Word in our hearts so that we may not sin against you or others.

Many Voices: **I am a student of your Word, Lord.**

One Voice: When my heart is breaking, I recite the Twenty-third Psalm. Your promise to walk with me through every valley sustains me.

Many Voices: **I am a student of your Word, Lord.**

One Voice: Find me, like Mary, Lord, sitting at your feet. Find me like Priscilla, Lois, and Eunice, Lord, eager to know your Word.

All Voices: **Lord, we are students of your Word. Open our hearts and minds that a fresh Word from you will strengthen our service to others.**

MEET 'N' GREET

Those Praying People
(Quickly match the name of these persons with their prayer petitions.)

1.	Daniel	A.	that his territory would be enlarged
2.	Hezekiah	B.	for daughters-in-law to find security
3.	Syrophoenician woman	C.	deliverance from Nebuchadnezzar's wrath
4.	Jesus	D.	to be spared the wrath of David and his men
5.	Paul and Silas	E.	to worship God in the Temple with fasting and praying

6. Thief on the Cross	F.	prayed to God three times a day
7. Moses	G.	for healing; granted fifteen more years of life
8. Elijah	H.	that her daughter would be healed
9. Shadrach, Meshach, and Abednego	I.	that the people with him would be sanctified in truth
10. Mary	J.	right to grant inheritance to daughters of Zelophehad
11. Jabez	K.	to be remembered by Jesus in paradise
12. Hannah	L.	for Peter to be delivered from jail
13. Abigail	M.	to have a son
14. Anna	N.	that it would not rain; it didn't for three and a half years
15. Naomi	O.	to praise God in prayer and song while in jail

Note: The answers to this match activity are in the *Leader's Guide* (online).

TEXT AND CONTEXT

Review Chapter 2 and your notes. If you are in a group, compile a corporate list from the assignment. Talk about the various contributions as you have time:

- Ten things that stand out
- Two ideas you would like to know more about
- Five things that evoke memories in your life (For example, someone may compare the "force of learning" like what happened in Antioch to what happened in their church when they used DISCIPLE Bible Study, or when they use the United Methodist Women Program Book. Someone else may name the persons who are like Barnabas and Lucy Rider Meyer in our churches, in our denomination.)

CLASS MEETING

Class Meeting (group)

1. Briefly answer the questions in the presence of one another:
   - How is it with your soul?
   - How have you studied God's Word this week?
   - What favorite scripture sustains your faith journey?
   - What book or author helps you learn God's Word?
2. Say a benediction:

   May God open our hearts and our minds so that we may be hearers and doers of God's Word. Amen. Amen.

Class Meeting (individual)

Answer these questions (aloud or writing in your journal):
   - How have you studied God's Word this week?
   - What favorite scripture sustains your faith journey?
   - What book or author helps you learn God's Word?

Also, consider answering these questions:
   - Do you [or your church] have a regular PRACTICE of study?
   - Do you have a PLACE of study (for example, at the beach, in a church building, a special place set aside at home)?
   - Do you have a PATTERN for study (a form of lection or liturgy)?

RESPOND AND REFLECT

Recall and tell the group your favorite story about Jesus (for example, when Zacchaeus meets Jesus).

Write or draw in your journal. Reflect on how you learn God's Word; write something that is important to you about the process of learning. Make a list of persons who have helped you on your faith journey and note significant milestones in your faith journey. You may also wish to record favorite Bible passages, sermons, books that have made an impact; list favorite Bible teachers.

CALL TO ACTION

Stay on Track: Continue memorizing the Memory Quote.

Put It on the Wall: Take a few sticky-notes and write down or draw something from the text or session to put on the wall. It could be a new learning, a scripture that is important to you, or a song that helps you "watch and pray."

Plan Your Work (group): On a single sheet of paper, write your name on one side of the paper, then turn it over and write an area of concern in your life and ministry at the top of the paper. One sentence is sufficient. You will be asked to help others also realize their ministry by adding a note of describing what to do, a book or website to read, a song to listen to, someone to talk to [see "An Example," below]. The idea is to support personal and societal transformation by gathering ideas and choosing a path of action. The study leader will guide you in receiving direction and support from classmates in addressing your ministry concern.

Plan Your Work (individual): Telephone or e-mail a friend and ask him or her to give you ideas about your ministry concern.

An Example
Sample Concern: My heart aches for youth who are aging out of the foster care system.
Sample Responses:
- The first person writes: Read Michael Oher's book, *I Beat the Odds*.
- The second person writes: Call your local foster care agency and volunteer to help.
- The third person writes: Have you heard of the Open Table movement for youth aging out of the foster care system?
- The fourth person writes: I am praying with you.

CLOSING WORSHIP

Song/Hymn

"Only Trust Him," *United Methodist Hymnal, #337*

Prayer

Lift up persons and institutions from the Prayer Calendar. Enter into silent prayer for them.

Then, read aloud this excerpt (volunteer):

> Sisters and brothers, through serious study and lively conversation, we enter with Jesus into the fray of life. Bible study must always be practical, always applicable to how we live, always producing in us, not only a spirit of openness to dialogue, but also a spirit of openness to action.

Learn Jesus Through *Lectio Divina*

Hear the story of Jesus from Luke 19:1-6. Read (or hear it read) three times.

This **first** time, listen for a word that summons your *attention*. Hear or read the scripture. After two full minutes of silence, record the word in your diary.

Listen to the story of Jesus for the **second** time: this time, identify an *emotion* that is evoked as you listen to the interchange between Jesus and Zacchaeus. Hear or read the scripture. After two full minutes of silence, write in your diary.

Listen for a **third** time. This time listen for an invitation to *do* something. Hear or read the scripture. After two full minutes of silence, write in your diary.

After everyone has finished writing, face another person and say the following declaration; or if you are studying individually simply recite the pledge aloud, beginning with "I pledge . . .":

My sister (or brother) in Christ, I pledge to grow in spiritual practices. I pledge to read my Bible, to use my devotional, and to hear God's words in response **magazine and other mission resources. And with God's help, I will obey God's commandment to love God and to love my neighbor as myself.**

ASSIGNMENTS

Read or review Chapter 3.
Write down ten things that stand out for you.
Identify ten people who have mentored you.
List ten significant spiritual events in your life.

Session 3: Mentor

WELCOME!

The goal of Session 3 is to delve into the experience of mentoring from biblical and current sociological perspectives, identifying key components that make mentoring successful and discovering ways in which mentoring strengthens the community of faith.

OBJECTIVES FOR THE SESSION

- To remember the hands and hearts that have guided us in our life
- To discuss key mentorships in the Bible
- To commit to helping others, even the not-so-perfect protégés

MEMORY QUOTE

[Based on Colossians 4:2-3]

Devote yourselves to prayer, keeping alert in it with thanksgiving. At the same time pray for us as well. Watch and pray!

GATHERING WORSHIP

Song/Hymn

"I Want Jesus to Walk with Me," *United Methodist Hymnal,* #521; or "In the Garden," *United Methodist Hymnal,* #314

Scripture (volunteer)
Acts 8:26-31

Prayer (volunteer)

Litany
One Voice (volunteer): If it had not been for the Lord on my side, where would I be? Where would I be?

Many Voices: **Lord, we thank you for being a "guide on the side."**

One Voice: You have sent teachers and preachers, encouragers and nurturers, briars and prodders so we can learn your way and do your will.

Many Voices: **Lord, thank you for those "guides on the side."**

One Voice: Open my eyes to any opportunity to speak a word of truth and hope to those around me. Teach me to be the "hand that guides," the mentor that supports, and the voice of wisdom and hope.

All Voices: **Lord, we have prayed, but we need your power. We have studied, but we need your strength. Make us able servants and guides to those who need your love in human form. Bless us that we may be a blessing. Amen.**

MEET 'N' GREET

Trace Your Hand (group): Use one sheet of construction paper to trace or draw a large hand. Cut out the hand. On one side, write the names of several people who have served as mentors in your life. On the reverse side, place the names of persons who have been "assigned to you" to mentor and guide. Your study leader will provide additional direction for this activity.

Trace Your Hand (individual): Trace and cut out several hands. On some of the hands, write the name (one name per hand) of a person who has served as a mentor to you. On other hands, write the name of a person whom you are mentoring. Place the hands on a wall or in your Bible. Make a commitment to pray for those persons and express thanks to your mentors in a tangible way.

TEXT AND CONTEXT

Review Chapter 3 and your notes. If you are in a group, compile a corporate list from the assignment. Talk about the various contributions as you have time:

- Ten things that stand out
- Two ideas you would like to know more about
- Five things that evoke memories in your life

Explore these questions:
- How have our homes, our churches, our schools served as a place for mentoring?
- What community organizations serve as mentoring forces (for example, Boys and Girls Club; The Links, Incorporated)?

CLASS MEETING

Class Meeting (group)
1. Answer these questions in the presence of one another:
- How is it with your soul?
- Who are your mentors? Who has guided you in your faith journey?
- Who are you mentoring and why?

2. Share a benediction:

> **May God grant us time and strength and courage to walk alongside those who need a friend. May we be beacons, lighthouses, flashlights—even a candle in the wind. We have heard the cry of the needy, and we are saying, "Send me, I'll go."**

Class Meeting (individual)

Answer these questions (aloud or writing in your journal):

- How is it with your soul?
- Who are your mentors? Who has guided you in your faith journey?
- Who are you mentoring and why?

Also, consider answering these questions:

- Do you [or your church] have a regular PRACTICE of mentoring or leadership?
- Do you have a PLACE for mentoring or leading?
- Do you have a PATTERN for developing leadership?

RESPOND AND REFLECT

Read the quote by John Wesley:

> **Make us faithful in all our contacts with our neighbors, that we may be ready to do good and bear evil, that we may be just and kind, merciful and meek, peaceable and patient . . . that so glorifying thee here we may be glorified with thee in thy heavenly kingdom.**[1]

Write or draw in your journal. Reflect on how you met your mentors, or how you selected someone (or someone selected you) to mentor; write the names of those you know who need a guiding hand, who need someone to show up in their lives to listen and pray with them.

CALL TO ACTION

Stay on Track: Continue memorizing the Memory Quote.

Volunteer for a team of three persons to navigate the "Stay on Track" game. Only this time one person steps on the words and that person is blindfolded (protégée). A second person serves as their mentor/guide (standing outside the rectangle); the mentor must give directions (for example, two steps to the left, four steps forward). The third person serves as the spoiler or distractor and tries to interfere with the progress. Afterward take time to discuss the experience.

Match the Mentor (group): Here are the names of some mentors and protégés. Match the mentor with the protégé as directed by your study leader: Philip/Eunuch; Elijah/Elisha; Barnabas/Paul; Moses/Joshua; Elizabeth/Mary; Kenny/Jack; Etta Barton/Chinsook Kwon; Sarah Ennalis/Henry Boehm; Maya Angelou/Oprah; Naomi/Ruth; Mordecai/Esther.

Match the Mentor (individual): Write a brief description in your journal about the connections between the mentor/protégé pairs you select from the above list.

Remember Your Faith Journey: Using a piece of construction paper, create a picture or written chart of your faith journey. Include eight to ten milestones, such as being confirmed, meeting a best friend, going to college, finding a church home, volunteering in mission, having children.

At the end of your faith journey, draw a circle and inside it draw or write what you see as your next opportunity. For example, someone could write the words "forever families" to signify the desire to continue to find families of the heart for young adults who have aged out of foster care systems and often have no consistent caring adults in their lives to guide them.

CLOSING WORSHIP

Song/Hymn
"God the Spirit, Guide and Guardian," *United Methodist Hymnal,* #648; "Send Me, Lord," *United Methodist Hymnal,* #497; or "How Shall They Hear the Word of God," *United Methodist Hymnal,* #649

Litany For Honoring Mentors
One Voice (volunteer): Let us remember that Elisha had Elijah, Paul had Barnabas, and Ruth had Naomi. Knowing that we do not journey alone, let us call out the names of our mentors and guides with thanksgiving.

Many Voices (several volunteers): _____, **I speak your name . . . thank you!**

One Voice: And in the same spirit, let us call forth by name (or concern) those to whom God has assigned us.

Many Voices (several volunteers): _____, **I am here for you.** (or) _____, **I am praying with you.**

All Voices: **Lord, we thank you for blessing us with your love and guidance. Thank you for our chance to pay it forward and pass it on!**

Declaration
> **Today, we pledge to be the one who reaches one. We pledge to be a shoulder to lean on and an ear attuned to hear. We pledge to break through the busyness of our lives, the struggle of our own pains, simply to say, "Here I am, neighbor; how can I serve you?"**

ASSIGNMENT

Read Chapter 4. Make note of key learnings and questions that may arise.

Session 4: Transform

WELCOME!

The goal of Session 4 is to hear the call to go forth and change the world, following the witness from biblical times as well as of modern-day workers for justice and peace. Stories found in **response** and *New World Outlook* magazines can highlight the work of those who have been transformed and seek to transform others as well.

OBJECTIVES FOR THE SESSION

- To examine the lives of persons who have prayed and planned for transformation of evil and unjust structures
- To hear anew the scripture's call on each believer's life to "do the right thing"
- To make a renewed commitment for advocacy in light of the fervor of John Wesley

MEMORY QUOTE

[Based on Colossians 4:2-3]
Devote yourselves to prayer, keeping alert in it with thanksgiving. At the same time pray for us as well. Watch and pray!

GATHERING WORSHIP

Song/Hymn
"I Am Thine, O Lord," *United Methodist Hymnal,* #419; or "Spirit of the Living God," *United Methodist Hymnal,* #393

Scripture (volunteer)
Isaiah 58:1-12

Prayer (volunteer)

Litany
One Voice (volunteer): Jesus calls us o'er the tumult of our life's wild, restless sea . . . asking us to follow him, to give our hearts to his obedience.

Many Voices: **Let my work, through you, be the change that someone needs.**

One Voice: Lord, you have come to the lakeshore; you need my hands full of caring, through my labors to give others rest.

Many Voices: **Let my work through you, be the change that someone needs.**

One Voice: We promise God, like the early disciples, to be change agents, to turn the world upside down, so that things can be RIGHT in this time and space.

All Voices: **Lord, I want to be a Christian in my heart. Lord, I want to be like Jesus in my heart. Lord, I want to be your eyes, hands, and feet. Transform the world through me.**

MEET 'N' GREET

TEXT AND CONTEXT

Review Chapter 4. Once again, identify

- Ten things that stand out
- Two ideas you would like to know more about
- Three things that evoke memories in your life

Explore this question:

- When you think of the call to transform, what people, events, or regions come to mind (for example, abortion, racial profiling, veterans services, civil war, fair wages, immigration, trafficking)?

CLASS MEETING

Class Meeting (group)

1. Answer the questions (choose one; give brief, one-minute responses):
   - How is it with your soul?
   - Brag on God: What is your testimony of transformation (either personally or someone else's life)?
   - What situation(s) are you longing to see transformed?
2. Share a benediction:

   May God give us wisdom and courage to do every day, everything that God has called us to do. May God make us willing and able. Amen.

Class Meeting (individual)

Answer these questions (aloud or writing in your journal):

- How is it with your soul?
- Brag on God: What is your testimony of transformation (either personally or someone else's life)?
- What situation(s) are you longing to see transformed?

Also consider the following questions:
- Do you or your community have a regular PRACTICE of transformation?
- Do you have a PLACE for seeking transformation?
- Do you have a PATTERN for transformation?

RESPOND AND REFLECT

Write or draw in your journal. Reflect on what situations hurt your heart and where you are committed to making changes, personally and corporately.

CALL TO ACTION

You will need a sheet of paper and a stamped envelope. Tear the paper in two. On one piece, create a vision sheet: list ways in which you will engage in personal transformation (such as, fasting, retreats, reading books, working with a life coach, serving in mission, and so forth).

On the second piece, create an action plan by listing areas of challenges and concerns that you plan to address within the next three months. You may list more than one item, but one is sufficient. Put a proposed date by each item on your action plan.

Write your address on the envelope, place your action plan inside, and seal the envelope. If you are in a group setting, give it to the study leader or a classmate, who will mail the envelope to you in three months. If you are doing this study as an individual, ask a friend to mail the envelope to you in three months. When you receive your action plan in three months, take time to match your vision and plans with your actions so far. Prayerfully, you will have made some strides in living out your vision for ministry.

CLOSING WORSHIP

Song/Hymn

"Change My Heart, O God," *The Faith We Sing*, #2152; "A Charge to Keep I Have," *United Methodist Hymnal*, #413; "The Summons," *The Faith We Sing*, #2130

Prayer (unison)

> Through these sessions, Lord, we have heard you calling our names. You have called us to pray like Hannah, lead like Deborah, mentor like Philip, and transform the world like Paul and Barnabas. May the Word and the words that have been sown in our hearts take root, flourish, and lead to our being a true disciple for you each and every day. Amen.

Litany

One Voice (volunteer): Will you come and follow Jesus if he but calls your name?

Many Voices: **I will, the Lord being my helper!**

One Voice: Will you regularly create time and space to pray?

Many Voices: **I will, the Lord being my helper!**

One Voice: Will you carefully learn Jesus through the study of the scripture?

Many Voices: **I will, the Lord being my helper!**

One Voice: Will you wisely mentor someone, whether familiar or unexpected?

Many Voices: **I will, the Lord being my helper!**

One Voice: Will you zealously transform pockets of injustice?

Many Voices: **I will, the Lord being my helper!**

One Voice: O God, as in biblical times, you have come to the lakeshore—this Mission u—looking for followers (not fans). We recommit ourselves to abstain from doing evil, to zealously do good works, and to constantly attend on all your ordinances.

Many Voices: **Lord, I have studied, but I need your strength. I have prepared, but I need your power. I am willing—and I want to—but only you can make me able. Silently now, I wait for thee, ready my God, thy will to see, open my eyes, illumine me, Spirit divine. Amen. Amen.**[1]

Endnotes

THIS IS *YOUR* GUIDE

1 "Class meetings, a part of Methodist history, have relevance today," by Linda Bloom, United Methodist News Service, 2004, http://archives.umc.org/interior .asp?ptid=2&mid=5937.

2 Code of Confidentiality and Conduct from Leader's Guide: *Poverty* © 2012 United Methodist Women. All rights reserved. Used by permission.

3 "United Methodists seek change in tone at assembly," August 3, 2007, United Methodist News Service, http://umc.org/site/c.lwL4KnNlLrH/b.3082929/apps/nl /content3.asp?content_id={2B1F5695-20AD-47C1-BAC7-18E6878B6063}&not oc=1#.UpAVVuI_SRM.

SESSION 1: PRAY

1 "Class meetings, a part of Methodist history, have relevance today," by Linda Bloom, United Methodist News Service, 2004, http://archives.umc.org/interior .asp?ptid=2&mid=5937.

SESSION 3: MENTOR

1 Donald Demaray, ed., *Devotions and Prayers of John Wesley* (Grand Rapids, MI: Baker Book House, 1959), 107.

SESSION 4: TRANSFORM

1 Sermon preparatory prayer used by Rev. Dr. Alyn Waller, pastor, Enon Baptist Church, Philadelphia, Pennsylvania, since 1988. Used by permission.

Bibliography

About John Wesley, A Scriptographic Booklet. Channing L. Bete Co., Inc.

"Class meetings, a part of Methodist history, have relevance today," by Linda Bloom. United Methodist News Service, 2004. http://archives.umc .org/interior.asp?ptid=2&mid=5937.

Spiritual Growth Study 2014: *How Is It With Your Soul?* by Jack Levison and Priscilla Pope-Levison. United Methodist Women, 2014.

"The Comparative Study: The Class Meeting of John Wesley and the Home Cell Group of Yonggi Cho," by Sin Ho Kim (Ph.D. candidate at Drew University). Presented at the 43rd Annual Meeting of the Wesleyan Theological Society. www.*wesley.nnu.edu/fileadmin/imported_site/wts/... /wtsfinalsinhokim.doc.*

About the Author

Faye Wilson is a frequent contributor to the mission studies of United Methodist Women. She worked for twenty-one years in the area of mission education with the General Board of Global Ministries. In that role, she served on the Program Committee for Education for Mission, National Council of Churches, and helped oversee the creation of mission education resources in an ecumenical arena. She provided training for conference and district secretaries of global ministries, led *Global Praise* workshops, and visited and served in mission ministries in more than twenty countries. She taught in her first Mission u (formerly School of Christian Mission) in August 1982.

She is the author of several mission studies including *Cuba, Mexico, Living as Christians in a Violent Society, The Girl Under the Bridge* (for children), and *Exodus* (for youth), and has written (adult) leader's guides for *Vietnam, Cambodia,* and *Laos*; *Food and Faith*; and *Poverty*. She also created the poverty study DVD.

Faye works full-time as a parent/community specialist with Wicomico County Public Schools. In her local church, Mt. Zion UMC (Quantico, MD), she is president of her United Methodist Women unit, the adult Sunday school teacher, the minister of music (directing three choirs), and coordinator for the Zeal of Zion praise dance ministry.

She has an M.A. in journalism from New York University, a master's in theological studies from Drew Theological Seminary, and an Ed.D. in adult education from Columbia University.

Also Available

Spanish translation of *How Is It with Your Soul?* By Priscilla Pope-Levison and Jack Levison
ISBN: 978-1-940182-06-3
M3180
$10

Korean translation of *How Is It with Your Soul?* By Priscilla Pope-Levison and Jack Levison
ISBN: 978-1-940182-07-0
M3181
$10

response magazine, April 2014 focusing on "How is it with your soul?"

Place your order with:
United Methodist Women Mission Resources
1-800-357-9857
www.umwmissionresources.org

How Is It with Your Soul? webpage:
www.unitedmethodistwomen.org/soul